Health Care Issues, Costs and Access

HEALTH CARE COSTS: OUTLOOK AND OPTIONS

HEALTH CARE ISSUES, COSTS AND ACCESS

The Health Care Financial Crisis: Strategies for Overcoming an "Unholy Trinity"
Cal Clark and Rene McEldowney (Editors)
2001. ISBN 1-56072-924-4

Health Care Crisis in America
James B. Prince (Editor)
2006. ISBN 1-59454-698-4

A New Epidemic: Harm in Health Care-How to make Rational Decisions about Medical and Surgical Treatment
Aage R. Moller
2007. ISBN 1-60021-884-9

Decision Making in Medicine and Health Care
Partricia C. Tolana (Editor)
2008. ISBN 1-60021-870-9

Social Sciences in Health Care and Medicine
Janet B. Garner and Thelma C. Christiansen (Editor)
2008. ISBN 978-1-60456-286-6

Health Care Policies
Linda A. Bartlette and Ida F. Lawson (Editor)
2008. ISBN 978-1-60456-352-8

Handbook of Stress and Burnout in Health Care
Jonathon R.B. Halbesleben (Editor)
2008. ISBN 978-1-60456-500-3

Medicare Payment Policies to Physicians
Katherine V. Bergen (Editor)
2009. ISBN 978-1-60692-131-4

Health Care Costs: Outlook and Options
Raymond W. Inhurst (Editor)
2009. ISBN ISBN 978-1-60692-151-7

Health Care Issues, Costs and Access

Health Care Costs: Outlook and Options

Raymond W. Inhurst
Editor

Nova Science Publishers, Inc.
New York

For permission to use material from this book please contact us:
Telephone 631-231-7269; Fax 631-231-8175
Web Site: http://www.novapublishers.com

LIBRARY OF CONGRESS CATALOGING-IN-PUBLICATION DATA
Available upon request
ISBN: 978-1-60692-151-7

Published by Nova Science Publishers, Inc. ✢ New York

CONTENTS

PREFACE

The U.S. political system arguably is not particularly effective at addressing gradual long-term problems such as rising health care costs and aging. But the problems caused by rising health care costs are not just long-term ones. In fact, some of them are already having significant effects on various aspects of our society. Health care costs are already reducing workers' take-home pay to a degree that is both under-appreciated and at least partially unnecessary, consuming roughly a quarter of the federal budget, and putting substantial pressure on state budgets (mostly through the Medicaid program), thereby constraining funding for other governmental priorities. Identifying and addressing inefficiencies in the nation's health care system can yield significant benefits, even in the short term, and focusing attention on those effects that are already occurring may be helpful in developing the consensus necessary to make the needed changes.

In: Health Care Costs: Outlook and Options
Editor: Raymond W. Inhurst, pp. 1-57 ISBN 978-1-60692-151-7

Chapter 1

EVIDENCE ON THE COSTS AND BENEFITS OF HEALTH INFORMATION TECHNOLOGY*

Congressional Budget Office

PREFACE

Many people believe that health information technology (health IT) has the potential to transform the practice of health care by reducing costs and improving quality. In this paper, prepared at the request of the Chairman of the Senate Budget Committee, the Congressional Budget Office (CBO) examines the evidence on the costs and benefits of health information technology, possible barriers to a broader distribution and use of it in hospitals and clinicians' offices, and possible options for the federal government to promote use of health IT. In keeping with CBO's mandate to provide objective, impartial analysis, the paper makes no policy recommendations.

Stuart Hagen of CBO's Health and Human Resources Division and Peter Richmond, formerly of CBO, prepared the report under the supervision of Bruce Vavrichek and James Baumgardner. Keisuke Nakagawa provided able research assistance. The report benefited from comments by Tom Bradley, Robert Dennis, Keith Fontenot, Holly Harvey, David Moore, Robert Nguyen, Allison Percy, William Randolph, and Philip Webre, all of CBO. In addition, several briefings organized by the Health Information Management Systems Society provided

* Excerpted from Congressional Budget Office paper, dated May 2008.

helpful data. A number of outside reviewers also provided comments: Laura Adams of the Rhode Island Quality Institute, Mark Leavitt of the Certification Commission for Health Information Technology, David Cutler of Harvard University, Richard Hillestad of the RAND Corporation, and Douglas Johnston and Eric Pan of the Center for Information Technology Leadership. (The assistance of external reviewers implies neither responsibility for the final product, which rests solely with CBO, nor endorsement of the conclusions of CBO's analysis)

Leah Mazade edited the report, and John Skeen proofread it. Maureen Costantino designed and produced the cover and prepared the report for publication. Lenny Skutnik produced the printed copies, Linda Schimmel coordinated the print distribution, and Simone Thomas prepared the electronic version for CBO's Web site.

Peter R. Orszag
Director

The complexity of modern medicine exceeds the inherent limitations of the unaided human mind.

David M. Eddy (1990)

INTRODUCTION AND SUMMARY

Information plays a key role in health care. Providers such as physicians and hospitals generate and process information as they provide care to patients. Managing that information and using it productively pose a continuing challenge, particularly in light of the complexity of the U.S. health care sector, with its many different types of providers, services, and settings for care. Health information technology (health IT) has the potential to significantly increase the efficiency of the health sector by helping providers manage information. It could also improve the quality of health care and, ultimately, the outcomes of that care for patients.

The term "health IT" generally refers to computer applications for the practice of medicine. Those applications may include computerized entry systems for physicians' ordering of tests or medications, support systems for clinical decisionmaking, and electronic prescribing of medications. (The appendix provides more information about the different types of health IT and the terminology used in the field.) Some or all of those components are housed in the electronic medical record (EMR). The electronic health record (EHR) is the primary health IT package commonly purchased by a provider. It is an EMR with the capacity to send and receive data electronically and meets the requirements for interoperability[1]. When used effectively, EHRs can enable providers to deliver health care more efficiently. For example, they can:

- Eliminate the use of medical transcription and allow a physician to enter notes about a patient's condition and care directly into a computerized record; [2]
- Eliminate or substantially reduce the need to physically pull medical charts from office files for patients' visits;
- Prompt providers to prescribe generic medicines instead of more costly brand-name drugs; and
- Reduce the duplication of diagnostic tests.

The adoption and proper use of EHRs could also improve the quality of health care. Among other things, they could:

- Remind physicians about appropriate preventive care;
- Identify harmful drug interactions or possible allergic reactions to prescribed medicines, and
- Help physicians manage patients with complex chronic conditions.

Many analysts and policymakers believe that health IT is a necessary ingredient for improving the efficiency and quality of health care in the United States. Despite the potential of health IT to increase efficiency and improve quality, though, very few providers—as of 2006, about 12 percent of physicians

---

[1] Interoperability describes the capacity of one health IT application to share information with another in a computable format (that is, for example, not simply by sharing a PDF [portable document format] file).

[2] Many physicians use voice dictation to document and report the results of examinations and procedures. Medical transcription is, in its simplest sense, the process whereby those dictated notes about a patient's care are converted into a typewritten format)

and 11 percent of hospitals— have adopted it.[3] An important question for policymakers, therefore, is whether—and if the answer is yes, how—the federal government should stimulate and guide the adoption of health IT.

Box 1. The Office of the National Coordinator of Health Information Technology

The Office of the National Coordinator of Health Information Technology (ONC) manages the federal government's activities in two main areas: the development of standards necessary to achieve the inter- operability of the large number of varying applications of health information technology (health IT) and the facilitation of information exchange.

Developing Standards to Ensure Interoperability

To establish processes for identifying standards with which health IT systems must comply and for certifying that the standards are being met, the Department of Health and Human Services (HHS), through ONC, set up the Health Information Technology Standards Panel (HITSP). The panel's overarching task is to promote interoperability in health care— the ability of systems and applications to communicate with each other. HHS also awarded a three-year contract to the Certification Commission for Healthcare Information Technology (CCHIT) to develop and evaluate certification criteria and create an inspection process for health IT.

As the standards process is currently set up, the HITSP develops industrywide health IT standards and recommends them to the Secretary of Health and Human Services, who first "accepts" them and then one year later officially "recognizes" them for use in federal health IT applications. (Such applications example, in the Veterans Health Administration— and by federal contractors.) The panel uses the one- year period to refine the instructions given to vendors for complying with the standards. The standard-setting process is designed to minimize the number of unworkable standards that are issued rather than to maximize the speed with which standards are set. Private-sector health IT users are not required to comply with the federal standards; nevertheless, the federal standards have become the de facto industry measure for achieving interoperability.

---

[3] Rates of adoption vary by the definition of health IT used in a particular survey. The rates given here are based on the adoption of health IT systems that include all or most recommended functionalities—such as electronic documentation of providers' notes, electronic viewing of laboratory and radiological results, electronic prescribing, computerized physician order entry, clinical decision support, and interoperability.

Health IT vendors who wish to have their products certified as compliant with new federal standards can submit those products for examination by CCHIT. Certified electronic health record products should be able to communicate and operate with other similarly certified systems.

Facilitating Health Information Exchange

To ease the electronic exchange of health-related information, HHS funded the creation of prototypes for organizing the components of the National Health Information Network (NHIN). ONC describes the NHIN as a "network of networks," built out of state and regional health information exchanges (and other networks) to link those various networks and the systems they in turn connect. The NHIN's mission is to develop a national capability to exchange standards-based health care data in a secure computer environment.

The Bush Administration has set the goal of making an EHR available for most Americans by 2014. In 2004, it established the position of the National Coordinator for Health Information Technology in the Department of Health and Human Services to help bring about the broad adoption of health IT (see Box 1).

Other federal agencies that finance health care or provide it directly have also taken steps to encourage adoption or to use health IT in their own clinical operations. Proposals before the Congress would expand the federal government's current activities by, among other things, mandating the use of some types of health IT, such as electronic prescribing ("e-prescribing"); offering financial incentives to providers who use health IT; and increasing the funds available for grants to purchase systems for providers.

This Congressional Budget Office (CBO) paper focuses on evidence about the benefits and costs of health IT and identifies and analyzes barriers to its adoption. Research indicates that in certain settings, health IT appears to make it easier to reduce health spending if other steps in the broader health care system are also taken to alter incentives to promote savings. By itself, the adoption of more health IT is generally not sufficient to produce significant cost savings.

The most auspicious examples involving health IT have tended to involve relatively integrated health systems. For example, Kaiser Permanente is a large staff-model health maintenance organization (HMO); the health plan and hospitals are jointly owned, and the providers work for the organization. For such a plan, reducing the number of unnecessary office visits (for patients' concerns or issues that could be handled to their satisfaction through telephone or e-mail consultations), for example, benefits the providers, the health plan, and the patients: It may lower the HMO's costs for providing health care—and thus improve the plan's "bottom line"—while minimizing inconvenience for patients. Kaiser has implemented a systemwide EHR in its facilities in some regions. In those areas, physicians have used such consultations to reduce the number of unnecessary office visits (compared with the number in regions without electronic systems).

A number of integrated delivery systems, including Intermountain Healthcare, Geisinger Health System, and Partners HealthCare, have also implemented EHRs across their organizations, and officials believe that as a result the systems have improved the efficiency and quality of the care they provide.[4] Some integrated systems have worked with health IT for decades. Intermountain Healthcare and the Department of Veterans Affairs (VA), for example, both began using computers to help manage clinical data in the 1970s. The VA has successfully implemented a systemwide EHR in a health care system that serves nearly 6 million patients in more than 1,400 hospitals, clinics, and nursing homes (Department of Veterans Affairs, 2008). According to the agency, its use of health IT has reduced its costs and greatly improved the quality of its care. (A recent Congressional Budget Office report [2007a] discusses the VA system in greater detail.)

For providers and hospitals that are not part of integrated systems, however, the benefits of health IT are not as easy to capture, and perhaps not coincidentally, those physicians and facilities have adopted EHRs at a much slower rate. Office-based physicians in particular may see no benefit if they purchase such a product—and may even suffer financial harm. Even though the use of health IT could generate cost savings for the health system at large that might offset the EHR's cost, many physicians might not be able to reduce their office expenses or increase their revenue sufficiently to pay for it.

For example, the use of health IT could reduce the number of duplicated diagnostic tests. However, that improvement in efficiency would be unlikely to increase the income of many physicians because laboratories and imaging centers typically perform such tests and are paid separately by health insurance plans. In cases in which a physician performs certain diagnostic tests in the office, reducing the number of duplicated tests would reduce his or her income. As a result, the capacity to avoid duplicating tests might not spur many physicians to invest in and implement a health IT system. Indeed, physicians might have a more powerful

[4] Those organizations are not integrated to the same extent as Kaiser. In general, the plans' providers are salaried employees or act in close partnership with hospitals and one another. They are affiliated with a health plan that covers a substantial percentage of their patients, but they also treat a large number of patients who are insured through other, nonaffiliated plans.

financial incentive to purchase additional office diagnostic equipment, for example, than to purchase a health IT system.

The search for improved efficiency in delivering health care has prompted numerous proposals for increasing the adoption of health IT. Two recent studies, one by the RAND Corporation and one by the Center for Information Technology Leadership (CITL), have estimated that about $80 billion in net annual savings is potentially attributable to such technology. Those studies have received significant attention, but for a number of reasons they are not an appropriate guide to estimating the effects of legislative proposals aimed at boosting the use of health IT. To take the RAND study as an example:

- The RAND researchers attempted to measure the potential impact of widespread adoption of health IT—assuming the occurrence of "appropriate changes in health care"—rather than the likely impact, which would take account of factors that might impede its effective use. For example, health care financing and delivery are now organized in such a way that the payment methods of many private and public health insurers do not reward providers for reducing costs— and may even penalize them for doing so.
- The RAND study was based solely on empirical studies from the literature that found positive effects for the implementation of health IT systems; it excluded the studies of health IT, even those published in peer- reviewed journals, that failed to find favorable results. The decision to ignore evidence of zero or negative net savings clearly biases any estimate of the actual impact of health IT on spending.
- The RAND study was not intended to be an estimate of savings measured against the rates of adoption that would occur under current law, but rather against the level of adoption in 2004. That is, the researchers did not allow for growth in adoption rates that would occur without any changes in policy, as CBO would do in a cost estimate for a legislative proposal.

One significant potential benefit of health IT that has thus far gone relatively unexamined involves its role in research on the comparative effectiveness of medical treatments and practices. Widespread use of health IT could make available large amounts of data on patients' care and health, which could be used for empirical studies that might not only improve the quality of health care but also help make the delivery of services more efficient.

By making clinical data easier to collect and analyze, health IT systems could support rigorous studies to compare the effectiveness and cost of different treatments for a given disease or condition. Then, in response to the studies' findings, they could aid in implementing changes in the kinds of care provided and the way those services were delivered, as well as track progress in carrying out the changes. Such comparative effectiveness studies could lead to reductions in total spending for health care because of the tendency in the current health care system to adopt ever more expensive treatments despite the lack of solid evidence about their effectiveness. The likelihood of such reductions in spending could be increased if the studies' findings were linked to the payments that providers received or the cost sharing that patients faced, particularly if sufficiently strict cost-effectiveness thresholds were used (Congressional Budget Office, 2007b).

If the federal government chose to intervene directly to promote the use of health IT, it could do so by subsidizing that use or by imposing a penalty for failing to use a health IT system. From a budgetary perspective, the subsidization approach is less likely than a penalty to generate cost savings for the federal government because of the costs of the subsidies: Payments would end up going to those providers who would have adopted a health IT system even without a subsidy as well as those providers for whom the subsidy made the difference in their decision to adopt one. However, providers may respond differentially to a subsidy or a penalty depending on how those interventions are presented.

EVIDENCE ON THE ADOPTION OF HEALTH INFORMATION TECHNOLOGY

A well-functioning EHR—comprising electronic documentation of providers' notes, electronic viewing of laboratory and radiological results, e-prescribing, and an interoperable connection via a health information exchange with all other providers and hospitals in a community—could have a significant impact on medical practice (Jha and colleagues, 2006). For example, consider a physician without a health IT system. The physician has a paper chart for each patient, and the following steps may then be involved in the patient's care:

- For each visit, the physician writes notes in the chart—or dictates them for later transcription—about the patient's condition and treatment. The nurse who takes the patient to the exam room records vital statistics (pulse, blood pressure, and temperature) in the paper chart. The physician writes out any needed prescriptions and gives them to the patient to fill at a pharmacy. If the chart contains information on the patient's allergies, the physician might check it to make sure the prescribed drug will have no adverse effects.

- If the physician decides to refer the patient to a specialist for a consultation, a portion of the patient's chart will go to that provider in the form of a letter. In many instances, however, the specialist does not receive a letter and has no information other than what might be noted in a referral form. The patient must then fill out a medical history and other forms required by the specialist. Moreover, unless the referring physician includes results from recent lab and radiology procedures, the specialist may well order similar diagnostic tests. If the physicians are both part of a multispecialty medical group that sees patients in multiple locations, the entire medical chart may need to be delivered to the specialist's office for the visit, risking the loss of the chart.
- Following the patient's visit, the specialist sends a letter back to the referring physician, detailing the results of the encounter. If the condition is serious, the specialist will probably communicate by telephone.

By contrast, consider a physician who uses an EHR. In that case:

- The physician might use a "drop-and-click" menu to note some elements of the patient's condition, reducing the need for handwriting or dictation and eliminating the delay—typically at least a week—in getting the transcribed notes into the chart.
- The EHR would automatically check any prescriptions for errors in dosing, allergies, and drug interactions; if the patient's health insurance plan included a formulary (a list of prescription drugs approved for use), the physician could discuss information about prices and copayments while the patient was still in the office. The EHR might also have a feature that could suggest a drug that might be a better choice, given the specifics of the patient's condition. The prescription would then be delivered electronically to the patient's pharmacy.
- A referral to a specialist would also be handled electronically. The clinical information necessary for the visit to the specialist would be automatically transmitted to that office and would include the results of any diagnostic procedures that the referring physician had ordered, including digitized images from radiological procedures.

- Following the consultation with the specialist, that physician's notes and recommendations would be electronically transmitted back to the referring physician's office, where they would become part of the patient's chart. Ideally, the EHR would substantially simplify operations in physicians' offices; it would have a similar if not a stronger impact in hospitals, given their more complicated care and treatment regimens.

As interest in health IT has grown, several surveys have attempted to measure current levels of its adoption.

- A survey sponsored by the Robert Wood Johnson Foundation (and summarized in Jha and colleagues, 2006) estimated that 24 percent of office-based physicians used an EHR of one type or another.[5] Physicians who worked in solo practices were less likely to have a health IT system than were physicians who worked in larger offices (adoption rates of 16 percent versus 39 percent, respectively).
- A 2006 survey of nonfederal office-based physicians by the National Center for Health Statistics reported that 12.4 percent of them used a comprehensive health IT system, and an additional 16.8 percent said they used some type of system[6]
- Another study, by the Center for Studying Health System Change, compared rates of health IT adoption for two periods: 2000 to 2001 and 2004 to 2005. The study found that adoption of health IT by large practices continued to exceed adoption by smaller practices by as much as 38 percentage points (Grossman and Reed, 2006).

The rates of adoption of EHRs by hospitals appear to be similar to those of physicians, according to recent analyses:

- Although the Robert Wood Johnson Foundation study mentioned above did not estimate the prevalence of EHRs in hospitals (because the available evidence was too limited), it concluded that only 5 percent of hospitals used computerized physician order entry (CPOE) systems, which are a key component of hospital EHRs (George Washington

[5] The full report of the survey is at www.rwjf.org/files/publications/ other/EHRReport0609.pdf.

[6] In the survey, reported by Hing, Burt, and Woodwell in 2007, an EMR system was deemed comprehensive if respondents answered "yes" to questions about computer applications for ordering prescriptions and tests and for test results and clinical notes.

University, Massachusetts General Hospital, and Robert Wood Johnson Foundation, 2006) [7]

- That conclusion is consistent with the findings of a 2005 study by Cutler, Feldman, and Horwitz, which found that 4 percent of hospitals were in full compliance with standards for CPOE, although an additional 17 percent of hospitals had made progress toward obtaining the technology. The Cutler team concluded that hospitals' profitability was not associated with the use of CPOE—a possible reason for the low adoption rates.
- A more recent survey by the American Hospital Association, reported in 2007, found that 11 percent of nonfederal hospitals had fully implemented EHRs. Such hospitals were more likely to be large urban or teaching hospitals than to be small community facilities.

Some international comparisons are available that measure investment in health IT and other parameters, such as rates of adoption and the functionalities that implemented systems provide. That research suggests that the United States lags behind other Western countries (specifically, the United Kingdom, Germany, Australia, the Netherlands, and New Zealand) although perhaps not dramatically, if the measure being used is the adoption of sophisticated IT systems. In several of those countries, rates of adoption of health IT systems among physicians are at or above 80 percent (Schoen and others, 2006). Although the data show that U.S. physicians are far less likely than physicians in those countries to use EHRs in their offices, they are just as or even more likely to use more-sophisticated electronic functions—such as accessing their patients' records remotely. That finding points to the difficulty of comparing rates of adoption—some countries may report high rates, but it is not clear whether their systems are particularly sophisticated or fully utilized (Schoen and others, 2006). In most countries in which rates of adoption are high, the government has heavily subsidized the acquisition of health IT systems by providers (Anderson and others, 2006)[8]

---

[7] Computerized physician order entry systems are electronic applications that physicians use to order medications, diagnostic tests, and other services.

[8] Some analysts point to those trends as indicating that the U.S. government could increase adoption of health IT systems through subsidization but that such support would not necessarily result in the adoption or use of those systems' more sophisticated features. See the later discussion on the question of a potential role for the federal government in speeding adoption of health IT.

EVIDENCE ON THE BENEFITS OF ADOPTING HEALTH INFORMATION TECHNOLOGY

No aspect of health IT entails as much uncertainty as the magnitude of its potential benefits. Some analysts believe that the adoption of such systems could provide substantial savings by lowering the cost of providing health care, eliminating unnecessary health care services (such as duplicate diagnostic tests), and improving the quality of care in ways that might reduce costs (by diminishing the likelihood of adverse drug events, for example). Other analysts expect little effect on costs but some improve ment in the quality of care. Another school of thought holds that health IT could bolster the quality of care but also increase expenditures on health care services — because improvements in quality would stimulate demand for additional services.

Wider adoption of health IT has the potential to generate both internal and external savings:

- Internal savings are those that can be captured by the provider or hospital that purchases the system; they are most likely to be in the form of reductions in the cost of providing health care—that is, improvements in the efficiency with which providers and hospitals deliver care.
- External savings are those that the provider or hospital that purchases the system cannot realize but that accrue to another such provider or perhaps the relevant health insurance plan or even the patient. Such savings might arise, for example, from the newfound ability of participants in the health care sector to exchange information more efficiently.

For integrated systems (such as Kaiser Permanente and the VA), more savings are internal than would be the case for providers that are not part of an integrated system. For example, integrated systems often have contracts with health insurance plans entailing that the systems assume the financial risk for the cost of prescription drugs and diagnostic tests, among other things, for the patients covered by those plans. As such, the systems can capture the savings from shifting their prescribing patterns toward generic drugs and reducing the number of duplicated diagnostic tests.

Different reimbursement arrangements might also shift savings from the external to the internal category in instances in which a provider is not part of an integrated system. A provider who was not affiliated with an integrated system but who treated HMO patients might be similarly rewarded for appropriate formulary management, which would shift those savings from being external to internal. But if the provider was paid purely on a fee-for-service basis, the savings would remain an external benefit.

The extent to which the use of health IT generates savings and how those savings are distributed across the health care sector can greatly influence the speed of broader adoption and use of those technologies. If health IT's adoption primarily produced internal savings for the providers and hospitals that purchased the systems— that is, if the purchasers of the systems were able to capture most of the cost savings that arose from using the technology—then the adoption of health IT would probably proceed apace without any need for intervention by the federal government. But if health IT appeared primarily to provide external savings—that is, if those who adopted the systems were unable to garner a sizable share of the benefits—then the adoption of such systems might proceed very slowly without additional governmental support.

Of the research to date, most studies examine how health IT might make the delivery of health care services more efficient, and they tend to focus on a particular clinical practice or area of potential savings. The evolving nature of the U.S. health care marketplace and of health IT has made it difficult to apply the results of such research to national estimates of the impact of health IT on the costs and quality of care. The few studies that have attempted to do so appear to have substantial shortcomings that limit their usefulness in analyzing legislative proposals. And some potential areas of research and analysis remain largely unexamined. They include the ways in which the delivery of health care services might change in response to the efficiencies that health IT offers and how the large amounts of clinical data available through EHRs could contribute to analyses of the comparative effectiveness and cost-effectiveness of different treatments.

Underlying any consideration of the potential benefits of health IT are the financial incentives that influence the behavior of health care providers, hospitals, health insurance plans, and patients. The use of information technology might lead to greater efficiency in delivering health care and to higher-quality services, but financial incentives could constrain many of those positive changes. For example, EHRs could provide physicians with a useful tool for reducing the number of unnecessary or duplicated laboratory tests that they ordered, but the likelihood of such reductions could depend on factors such as whether physicians were compensated for controlling the use of laboratory testing (as in some managed care plans) or whether they derived income from ordering more tests. How well health IT lives up to its potential depends in part on how effectively financial incentives can be realigned to encourage the optimal use of the technology's capabilities.

A general indication of health IT's usefulness in improving efficiency and quality can be seen in the adoption of such applications by integrated health care delivery systems (such as staff-model HMOs). By their nature, those types of systems are able to garner more of the benefits of health IT than nonintegrated providers can. Not surprisingly, such entities have relatively high rates of adoption of health IT.

Estimates of the Potential National Savings from Widespread Adoption of Health IT

Two studies, one by the RAND Corporation and one by the Center for Information Technology Leadership, report estimates of the potential net benefits that could arise nationwide if all providers and hospitals adopted health information technology and used it appropriately. (For the RAND research, see Girosi, Meili, and Scoville, 2005; and Hillestad and others, 2005. The CITL study is reported by Walker and colleagues, 2005, and Pan and others, 2004.) Both studies estimated annual net savings to the health care sector of about $80 billion (in 2005 dollars), relative to total spending for health care of about $2 trillion per year. The studies, however, measured different sources of such savings. The RAND research focused primarily on savings that the use of health IT could generate by reducing costs in physicians' practices and hospitals, whereas the CITL study limited its scope to savings from achieving full interoperability of health IT, explicitly excluding potential improvements in efficiency within practices and hospitals.

Neither the RAND nor the CITL study, however, is an appropriate guide to the budgetary effects of legislative proposals aimed at increasing the use of health IT. For example, both studies attempt to measure the potential impact of widespread adoption of health IT, not the likely impact; a CBO cost estimate, by contrast, would estimate the likely effect. And whatever the net savings to the health care system as a whole, the impact on the federal budget would be far smaller than that. Medicare and the federal share of Medicaid together account for only about one-fourth of total spending for health care services. Moreover, some types of savings, such as those from improved efficiency within a physician's office, could not be realized by Medicare without revising payment rates to physicians, which usually requires legislation. There are also other reasons, discussed in detail below, that the studies are not appropriate for estimating the impact of a legislative proposal. The bottom line is that both studies appear to significantly overstate the savings for the health care system as a whole—and by extension, for the federal budget—that would accrue from legislative proposals to bring about widespread adoption of health IT.

The RAND Analysis. The RAND analysis itself notes that its estimate is of health IT's potential savings and costs: "We use the word potential to mean 'assuming that interconnected and interoperable EMR systems are adopted widely and used effectively [emphasis added].' Thus, our estimates of potential savings are not predictions of what will happen but of what could happen with HIT [health information technology] and appropriate changes in health care [emphasis added]" (Hillestad and others, 2005, p. 1104). By incorporating the assumption of "appropriate changes in health care," the study's estimate deliberately does not take into account present-day payment incentives that would constrain the effective utilization of health IT, even if the technology was widely adopted. A key reason for the currently low rate of adoption of health IT may be that, given the way health care financing and delivery are now organized, the payment methods of both private and public health insurers in many cases do not reward providers for reducing some types of costs—and may even penalize them for doing so. Most providers are paid on a fee-for-service basis; if they were to reduce health care costs by providing fewer or less expensive services, they would have to submit lower charges to insurers, and as a result, their payments would decline. If technologies were adopted without changing those incentives, then the RAND estimate would be too high because the "appropriate changes in health care" assumed in the study would not have been made.

Another issue raised by the RAND study is that it was based solely on empirical studies from the literature that found positive effects for the implementation of health IT systems. Researchers offered this rationale: "We chose to interpret reported evidence of negative or no effect of HIT as likely being attributable to ineffective or not-yeteffective implementation" (Hillestad and others, 2005, p. 1105). However, a number of studies of health IT published in peer-reviewed journals have failed to find favorable results (for example, Garrido and others, 2005; Overhage and others, 2001). Consequently, the decision to ignore evidence of zero or negative net savings clearly biases—possibly quite substantially—any estimate of the actual impact of health IT on spending.

The methods researchers used in the RAND study would not be appropriate for assessing the savings that a legislative proposal would generate because, unlike the procedures used for a CBO cost estimate, savings were not measured relative to a current-law baseline. Instead, RAND researchers used the level of health IT adoption in 2004 as a baseline and assumed for comparison purposes that adoption remained at that level during the period over which they projected savings. A CBO cost estimate, however, would reflect the continuing growth in health IT adoption that would occur without any change in law. To the extent that health IT adoption has grown since 2004 and will continue to grow, that growth reduces the possible cost savings, compared with RAND's estimate, that could come about by encouraging wider adoption.

In several specific parts of the RAND analysis, the savings that would accrue from widespread adoption of health IT appear to be overstated. For example, it is likely that the RAND researchers significantly overestimated savings for health IT from reductions in the average length of stay in a hospital.[9] The RAND researchers assumed that reductions in lengths of stay would result in proportional reductions in costs. They noted, though, that health IT would primarily reduce lengths of stay by speeding up how quickly procedures were performed. If that is the primary channel through which lengths of stay are reduced, at least some costs will simply be shifted to earlier days in the stay and not eliminated—which argues for a reduction in costs that is less than proportional to the reduction in the average length of stay.[10]

The RAND estimate also failed to take into consideration that hospitals often achieve reductions in their averagelength-of-stay measures by shifting patients to another health care site, such as a skilled nursing facility. That practice produces fewer net savings because although such shifts reduce costs in the hospital sector, they increase them in the skilled-nursing sector.

---

[9] The study also makes what are probably optimistic assumptions about the savings from more efficient use of prescription drugs (for example, from switching to generic medications). It relies on the results of three studies of the effects of health IT on drug utilization, each of which has significant drawbacks. Two of the studies were conducted by a private consulting firm and were not published in a peer-reviewed journal; one of those studies was based on the experiences of only one clinic, and the other was an estimate of potential savings from using a particular vendor's e-prescribing product. The third study was based on the opinions of an expert panel, which estimated savings only for capitated plans and not for fee-for-service plans. (In capitated plans, providers give specified services to patients for a fixed monthly fee, regardless of the amount of care each patient actually receives.) The RAND researchers implicitly assumed that savings in the feefor-service sector would be the same as those in the capitated sector. That assumption probably overstates the impact of the use of health IT because it ignores the very different set of economic incentives that capitated providers face compared with those faced by providers who are paid on a fee-for-service basis.

[10] Furthermore, the estimate of the reduction in the average length of stay was based on the average reduction reported in three studies. Two of them were single-hospital case studies that reported very different reductions—5 percent and 30 percent—in average stays; the third study was based on data from 1996, a period during which hospitals were significantly reducing their costs per admission in response to pressures from the spread of managed care. Today, more than 10 years after hospitals first experienced such forces, it is unlikely that additional savings would be as easy to obtain as they were during that earlier period.

Another issue raised by the RAND analysis is the method that the researchers used to estimate savings from eliminating or reducing the use of paper medical records: They based their findings on the experiences of recent adopters of electronic medical record systems and then applied the savings to all physicians' offices. Yet that assumption might not be realistic for small practices (those that have fewer than four practitioners) because the same person who pulls charts in those offices typically also schedules appointments, administers billing, and performs other administrative tasks. Thus, although the overall workload of such staff might be diminished, those practices would find it difficult to reduce their costs by eliminating support staff positions. About half of physicians are in small practices; consequently, RAND's estimate of savings in this area is probably overstated.

Finally, the RAND study did not consider the broader impact that reducing at least some types of health care costs would have on the utilization of services. If the widespread use of health IT reduced the cost of health care services, that decline would eventually be reflected in lower prices and copayments for patients—and as prices fell, patients would demand more care. Even if the researchers' underlying assumptions about savings are accurate, the net effect of more use of health IT would probably still be lower overall costs than would otherwise be the case—but the reduction would not equal the amount that the RAND analysis has suggested.

The Study by the Center for Information Technology Leadership. Many of the same concerns raised by the RAND analysis apply to the study conducted by CITL. For one thing, the authors did not fully consider the impact of financial incentives in their analysis; they did not take into account the effect of those incentives on the use of health IT by providers, hospitals, and insurers or the effect on patients' demand for health care services in the event that health IT reduced the cost of care. The CITL analysis also estimated the $80 billion in potential savings against a baseline of little or no information technology use. Savings would come, the study suggests, by moving the U.S. health care sector from Level 1 (with completely nonelectronic data and with all information written down or shared verbally) to Level 4 (with all standardized machine-interpretable data). The impact of moving from the current level of adoption to Level 4 would be much smaller because many of the nation's health care providers already operate above Level 1 in their use of technology. (For example, Level 2 includes the use of fax machines, which are widely available in physicians' offices today.) As the report by Pan and others (2004) states, "the model [used in the study] does not account for the 'current state of affairs'" (p. 17).

Like the assumptions in the RAND analysis, some of those that the CITL study used appear to be overly optimistic:

- The CITL study estimated that the administrative cost of a laboratory test (encompassing both the provider's and the lab's expenses) was about $40 and that widespread interoperability could save about $38 per test—producing estimated national savings on lab tests of about $25 billion annually. However, the results of another analysis (Baker, 2005) raise doubts that the administrative cost of a lab test could possibly be as high as $40 to begin with.
- The CITL researchers assumed that fully interoperable health IT systems would eliminate 95 percent of avoidable tests, resting that assumption on the belief that physicians would choose to override the system's warnings on such tests only 5 percent of the time. Other estimates of avoidable tests typically report higher override rates, however (Bates and colleagues, 1999b).
- The CITL study also assumed that at the highest level of health IT adoption, only 0.001 percent of prescriptions would require a phone call between a pharmacist and a prescribing physician. Certainly, greater implementation of health IT could significantly reduce the number of those telephone calls, but the reduction that the CITL researchers assumed does not appear to be attainable.

Evidence on Improvements in Efficiency from Adoption of Health IT

The potential of health IT to reduce spending for health care depends in large part on its ability to make care more efficient by cutting the cost of delivering services, avoiding redundant services, and improving providers' productivity. Evidence from the literature on health IT, however, does not uniformly support the possibility of such savings. The potential for savings appears to depend heavily on their source and whether that source is in a hospital or in an ambulatory care setting (such as a clinic or a physician's office). In addition, savings are difficult to assess because the trimming of costs in one area of a physician's practice, for example, may be offset by increased costs or reduced efficiency in another area.

Estimating the impact of some potential sources of savings, especially those arising from greater exchange of information among providers, insurers, and patients, is especially difficult because health IT networks are in an early stage of development. Furthermore, health care providers and hospitals that were early adopters of health IT may have been motivated by particular characteristics of their organizations or operations that made them more likely than nonadopters to achieve benefits from health IT—in which case the outcomes they have seen might not be generalizable. Evidence of savings in the health care sector as a whole from adopting health IT is also limited.

Nevertheless, savings could accrue in a number of areas: the handling of medical records, the redundancy of diagnostic tests, the prescribing and use of drugs, the productivity of caregivers, and the length of hospital stays. Savings could also arise if a comprehensive interoperable health IT system, including a health information exchange that facilitated the sharing of health care information, was implemented.

Eliminating Paper Medical Records. Providers typically adopt EHRs with the intention of replacing their paper medical record systems. Research has shown that physicians' offices can realize savings from reducing the pulling of paper charts and the use of transcription services (Wang and others, 2003). Those savings might not apply in very small practices, however, because such offices typically have low but relatively fixed costs related to medical records and the physicians who work there are much more likely than those in larger practices to write notes manually in the charts. Savings from less pulling of charts is typically accomplished by reducing the number of staff required to do so. But that type of staff reduction may be impossible in a small practice if the employee who pulls charts also performs other tasks (such as scheduling and billing), as is usually the case.

The extent of savings to be gained from eliminating paper medical records would also depend on how well a physician used the new system. For example, most EHRs allow physicians to create templates that can significantly reduce the amount of time spent typing in notes, ordering medications, and so forth. But making effective use of templates and other features of EHRs would require a physician to make a substantial up-front investment in time to create templates suited to his or her style of practice and to learn how to use them effectively.

Moreover, many physicians would have to alter the way they practiced medicine to make a health IT system work for them, and not all physicians appear willing to make such changes. For example, some providers who have already installed EHRs continue to maintain paper charts; Miller and colleagues (2005) noted that 10 of 14 practices they examined stopped pulling charts—which implies that 4 practices still did not. Presumably, as physicians became more accustomed to the new electronic systems, they would stop using paper charts.

Avoiding Duplicated or Inappropriate Diagnostic Tests. The possibility of duplicating diagnostic tests arises when patients are seen by different physicians in multiple facilities or when records make it difficult to discern which tests have or have not been administered. Inappropriate testing can also occur because of a physician's habits or preferences, and a pattern of such testing may be easier to identify and change if information is in an electronic format. For the most part, any savings from avoiding duplicate or inappropriate diagnostic tests would be realized primarily by a health insurance plan, not a health care provider. Thus, the extent to which savings in this area would actually benefit providers is unclear.

Despite somewhat mixed results, most evidence suggests that EHRs have the potential to reduce the number of inappropriate laboratory tests. Bates and colleagues (1999b) found that providers canceled 69 percent of lab tests when alerted by an electronic notice that a test appeared to be redundant. That result, when combined with a related estimate that 9 percent of all lab tests appeared to be redundant (Bates and colleagues, 1998b), implies that EHRs with a notice of redundancy could reduce the number of laboratory tests by about 6 percent (69 percent of 9 percent). Consistent with this estimate, research by Tierney and others (1987) found that showing physicians information about a patient's previous lab work when they ordered a test in a clinic's order entry system and reminding them of the date of the patient's last test reduced the volume of tests ordered by about 6 percent. A second study reported by Tierney and colleagues in 1988 found a drop of about 9 percent in lab charges. The Tierney research, however, is based on data collected in the mid-1980s, and its applicability in today's health care environment is questionable.

By contrast, an evaluation of laboratory services in the outpatient facilities of two separate Kaiser Permanente regions that adopted health IT systems did not find a difference in the number of duplications as a result (Garrido and others, 2005). It is unclear what specific methods the systems used to prevent the duplication of tests and whether using the same methods shown to be effective in other studies would also have been effective for the Kaiser facilities. Moreover, as a fully integrated HMO, Kaiser may have already used non-health IT methods to reduce the number of unnecessary tests. For that reason, the results of the study may not be applicable to the non- HMO health care sector.

Reducing the Use of Radiological Services. Less information is available about the impact of EHRs on the use of radiological services. The Garrido team's 2005 study of Kaiser facilities also examined imaging and, as was the case with laboratory testing, found no change following the adoption of health IT. A study by Harpole and others (1997) found that providing physicians with evidence-based critiques of certain types of imaging at the point at which a provider orders a radiological study (that is, providing a clinical decision support system) had no significant effect on whether or not a test was ordered but did influence the types of radiological images that were taken. Health IT thus appears to ease the job of monitoring the use of radiological services, but there is little evidence that it helps control costs.

Promoting the Cost-Effective Use of Prescription Drugs. Evidence suggests that in hospitals, features of EHRs— specifically, clinical decision support (CDS) and computerized physician order entry—could help reduce the cost of prescription drugs by prompting providers to use generic alternatives, lower-cost therapies, and, for more complex drug regimens, cost-effective drug management programs (Mullett and others, 2001; Teich and others, 2000). In outpatient settings such as clinics and physicians' offices, health IT—specifically, e-prescribing— could alter prescribing practices in the direction of lower- cost drugs.[11]

Little empirical evidence exists, however, on the effectiveness of health IT to help manage the use of prescription drugs in either hospital or outpatient settings. One factor limiting cost savings is that physicians generally do not benefit financially from effectively managing the utilization of drugs. Instead, any financial gain is usually realized by health plans or pharmacy benefit management companies (PBMs). Moreover, because of their strong incentives to hold down costs, health plans and PBMs may already be capturing a substantial portion of those savings.

Improving the Productivity of Nurses and Physicians. Several analyses have investigated whether EHRs in hospitals and outpatient facilities might increase the productivity of nurses and physicians. A 2005 summary of research by Poissant and others suggests that when health IT systems were in use, nurses in hospitals saw drops in the time required to document the delivery of care but physicians saw increases in documentation time. That finding implies that hospitals might be able to reduce their spending on nurses but not necessarily on physicians. Those studies, however, may have identified a short-term effect among physicians—that is, before providers had become accustomed to the new system and incorporated the new methods into their daily routine. In addition, most studies have examined

[11] Wang and colleagues (2003) estimate that health IT systems in the offices of primary care physicians could save 15 percent of total drug costs per year in capitated plans, but that number is based on the opinions of an expert panel and not on actual data. Given that capitated plans already have a powerful incentive to encourage the use of less expensive drugs, an effect of 15 percent may be overly optimistic. Some research also indicates that some providers apparently have trouble using the prescribing functions in health IT systems (Wang and others, 2003; Grossman and others, 2007).

health IT in teach- ing hospitals, and the generalizability of their results to more typical community hospitals may be limited.

Few studies have measured the effect of EHRs on physicians' efficiency in outpatient settings, and those that have show mixed results (Pizziferri and others, 2005; Overhage and others, 2001). The lack of demonstrated gains in productivity as a result of implementing health IT systems may be partially due to some providers' tendency to duplicate the system's functions by continuing to do some tasks manually, such as maintaining paper records (Gans and others, 2005; Overhage and others, 2001). Physicians that eliminate or reduce their use of transcription services by adopting a health IT system may see savings, though. Intermountain Healthcare maintains that its savings from reducing transcription costs alone (as high as $12,500 per year for some physicians) contributed substantially to paying for its EHR, which cost about $2,500 per physician.[12]

The measures of productivity that researchers have used in such studies are relatively narrow and do not exhaust the ways in which the use of health IT might affect health care workers' productivity. For example, the improvements in documentation that EHRs provide might help physicians improve their caregiving: If such systems led providers to spend more time documenting the care they delivered, the end result might be higher-quality care. Health IT systems might also enable a physician to provide other services for patients, such as helping them get appropriate preventive care, providing better education about their health, and assisting them in making choices from among an array of treatment options.

Reducing the Length of Hospital Stays. Some research (Mekhjian and others, 2002) suggests that health IT could reduce the average length of a hospital stay by 5 percent or more by speeding up certain hospital functions (such as ordering and completing tests, ordering and administering medications, and collecting information and preparing for patients' discharge) and by avoiding costly errors (such as adverse drug reactions that could lead to delays in discharging patients). Other research has produced mixed results.

As discussed earlier with regard to the RAND study, reductions in the average length of hospital stays are unlikely to result in cost savings of a similar proportion to the reduction in average length of stay, such as that found by the Mekhjian research team (that is, of 5 percent or more). In particular, reductions in stays that stem from performing various hospital functions more quickly are not likely to cut costs as much as will reductions that result from improving care—for

[12] Personal communication to CBO from Len Bowes, Senior Medical Informaticist, Intermountain Healthcare, May 18, 2008; Clayton and others (2005).

example, by diminishing the number of adverse drug reactions. Reducing the length of time required to process a lab test or diagnostic image from the time it is ordered to the moment the results are delivered only speeds up the delivery of care; it does not necessarily reduce the amount of care provided or its associated cost.

Moreover, the promise of shortening the average length of time that a patient stays in the hospital might not be very compelling to a typical institution because it already faces a sizable financial incentive to pare its costs per admission. Payment incentives in the Medicare program that encourage hospitals to reduce their per admission costs have been in place since the early 1 980s; the average length of stay has fallen steadily since then, although recently, the downward trend has slowed (National Center for Health Statistics, 2007). In all likelihood, the majority of hospitals have already made most of the changes necessary to maximize their payments for the care of Medicare patients, and the additional money they would get from the next increment in reducing the average length of stay might not be worth the additional investment in health IT needed to produce it. Moreover, the payment methods for hospital stays that are common among private health plans—per diem payments (that is, a set fee per day in the hospital)—may work against shortening those stays.

Evidence on Improvements in the Quality of Care from Adoption of Health IT

The use of health IT applications has the potential to increase patients' safety within the overall health care system and improve the quality of the care that physicians and other caregivers provide. When used for prescribing medications, EHRs and their computerized physician order entry features can help prevent costly medical errors by checking patients' medical records and the list of medications they are taking, screening the list for possible drug allergies and drug interactions, and alerting physicians to any potential conflicts. The quality of health care could be improved through the use of clinical decision support systems to remind physicians to schedule tests, help diagnose complicated conditions, and more effectively implement appropriate protocols for treatment. In addition, the extensive data about patients that the use of EHRs generates might allow researchers to inform evidence-based guidelines and compare the effectiveness of different treatments for different patients as well as the effectiveness of different designs for the delivery of care.[13]

Like the benefits from delivering care more efficiently, however, benefits that stem from improving the quality of care—and the potential cost savings that accompany them—are primarily realized by patients and insurers rather than the providers who generally make the investment in health IT that leads to those benefits. Seldom are providers directly compensated for improvements in the quality of their care. Indeed, if those improvements, for example, cut down the number of hospitalizations and office visits, they might actually reduce a provider's compensation, especially in the case of providers paid on a fee-for-service basis (as is commonly the case). Improvements of that kind might enhance a provider's reputation and thereby attract more patients over the long run. But those outcomes would not necessarily increase a provider's income or lower his or her costs. (Also, some providers might discount the value of those benefits because they already had what they considered to be a sufficient number of patients and felt no need to add new ones.)

A possible benefit of improving care through the use of health IT, however, might be to lower malpractice insurance costs for providers. A number of firms that sell liability insurance for physicians are beginning to offer discounted premiums to practices that use EHRs.[14]

Avoiding Adverse Drug Events. One of the most common types of medical error—and a focus of much research—is a so-called adverse drug event, in which a patient has an adverse reaction from being administered an inappropriate medication. Research examining serious errors in the medications that patients receive in hospitals has shown that such mistakes are both common and potentially expensive and that they could be substantially reduced through greater use of health IT. Studies have found potential reductions in error rates from the use of health IT of between 50 percent and over 90 percent (Potts and others, 2004; Bates and others, 1 999a, 1 998a; Evans and others, 1998).[15] In a few other studies (Han and others, 2005; Nebeker and others, 2005; Upperman and others, 2005), researchers did not find that the rate of adverse drug events was lowered—although that result might have had more to do with the quality of the health IT systems being used than the performance of such systems in general.

---

[13] Evidence-based guidelines are recommended methods of treatment that are based on empirical research.

[14] Personal communication to CBO staff from Mark Leavitt, Executive Director, Certification Commission for Healthcare Information Technology, February 7, 2008.

[15] Not all serious medication errors, however, lead to adverse drug events. About 57 percent of all such errors have no adverse effect on the patient; they are often called "potential adverse drug events" (Bates and others, 1988a).

Much less evidence is available on how EHRs affect adverse drug events in outpatient settings. One study (Gandhi and others, 2005) found no evidence of reductions in such errors but qualified those findings by pointing out the lack of sophistication of the systems used by the physicians in the study.

By maintaining a list of a patient's allergies and current medications, a health IT system makes it easier for doctors to check for drug and drug-allergy interactions and for contraindications (stemming, for example, from the results of a laboratory test) to prescribing a particular medication. Health IT systems can also speed providers' access to lists of possible side effects of particular drugs, which allows physicians to quickly verify whether a drug is appropriate for a given patient. Most EHRs (with or without a CPOE feature) automatically check for allergy and drug interactions and for the appropriateness of a particular medication and warn the physician of potential conflicts. Such systems can also provide doctors with standardized dosing amounts or recommended dosing guidelines that can help prevent errors in overmedicating and undermedicating patients. Further, the automated prescribing practices possible with CPOE features may help reduce errors resulting from miscommunication among physicians, pharmacists, patients, and nurses.

Because medical errors can lead to the use of additional health care services, health IT systems that successfully reduce such errors may also diminish expenditures on health care. The effectiveness of health IT in reducing errors, however, depends largely on the type, setting, and quality of the systems. One study (Jha and others, 2001) found that 1.4 percent of hospital admissions were caused by adverse drug events, and 28 percent of those were considered preventable. The average cost of treating the consequences of a preventable adverse drug event, researchers estimated, was more than $10,000. Another study (Honigman and others, 2001) determined that adverse drug reactions that arose through care provided at an outpatient facility and that required hospitalization occurred at an average annual rate of 3.4 for every 1,000 patients. Avoiding even a fraction of the errors that now occur in inpatient and outpatient settings could yield significant savings.

Some of the potential savings from errors originating among outpatient providers, however, are probably already being realized by existing electronic systems. Even though today very few prescriptions (an estimated 7 percent in 2008) are handled exclusively through electronic means, some aspects of prescribing are almost universally electronic. For example, nearly all pharmacies connect electronically to health plans when they enter a patient's prescription into their computer system. At that point, the health plan has data on most if not all prescriptions that the patient has—and the pharmacist has that information through the health plan's system—and both the health plan's and the pharmacy's systems typically check for drug interactions and possible allergic reactions. (If a PBM is also involved, it may undertake some checking as well.) A provider's health IT system might still contribute to improving the quality of a particular patient's care if, for example, the patient had a result from a recent lab test that might suggest something about his or her response to a particular medication—although it is becoming more common for health plans also to have access to lab results (SureScripts, 2007).

Expanding Exchanges of Health Care Information. The adoption of interoperable health IT systems could ease exchanges of health care information, which might not only improve the quality of care but also reduce costs. The effects of expanding such exchanges include:

- Lessening the duplication of diagnostic procedures (because results could more easily be made available to other providers);
- Preventing medical errors (because providers would have more accurate and more complete information about the patients they are treating); and
- Lowering administrative costs (because automated transfers of test results, clinical information, and prescriptions among health insurers, physicians' offices, hospitals, laboratories, imaging facilities, pharmacies, and public health agencies would be less costly than manual transfers).

The realization of other benefits from greater exchange of information, such as the availability of more data for medical research, lies further in the future (see the later discussion).

An increased capability to exchange information is not sufficient, however, to reduce costs and improve the quality of health care because existing mechanisms for paying providers do not create incentives to reduce costs by acting on that information. Indeed, in some cases, those mechanisms create incentives that discourage efforts to cut costs. For example, a provider who is paid on a feefor-service basis might refrain from ordering a diagnostic test if the results of the same test recently ordered by another provider were in the patient's EHR (owing to health information exchange); however, that fee-forservice physician would have no financial incentive to do so. Moreover, if the physician could perform the diagnostic test in his or her office by using office-based equipment (such as an X-ray machine), the stronger financial incentive would be to ignore the previous test's results.

One potential source of empirical evidence on the benefits of health information exchange is the experience of integrated health systems that use systemwide EHRs— although separating out the impact of expanded information exchange from other health IT-related effects is difficult. The case of the VA illustrates some of the empirical challenges. The agency reports that its cost per patient has stayed relatively flat over the past several years, which it attributes in part to reducing the number of full-time- equivalent employees per 1,000 patients by 37 percent at the same time that the cost of medical care has been rising by about 6 percent per year (Evans, Nichol, and Perlin, 2006). After an adjustment for changes over time in the mix of patients that the VA sees, its spending per enrollee grew by a total of 1.7 percent in real terms from 1999 to 2005 (0.3 percent annually)—a rate significantly below Medicare's real rate of growth in costs per capita of 29.4 percent (4.4 percent per year) over the same period (Congressional Budget Office, 2007a).

Those results cannot be attributed solely to the impact of the VA's health IT program, however, because the VA differs in many ways from Medicare and other parts of the health system. In addition, the VA adopted other efforts to control costs during the 1999–2005 period; for example, it switched from a labor-intensive inpatient system to a system of outpatient clinics.

Expanding the Practice of Evidence-Based Medicine. Part of the motivation for the broader adoption of health IT has come from evidence of deficits in the quality of health care in the United States and large unexplained geographic variations in the utilization and cost of care (McGlynn and others, 2003; Congressional Budget Office, 2008).[16] Many health IT systems have some type of clinical decision support function—such as automated reminders about preventive care—that could help physicians adhere to evidence-based guidelines, avoid preventable errors, reduce the use of procedures that have no demonstrated clinical value, ultimately improve the quality of the care that they provide, and possibly cut costs. Measuring the effects of using clinical decision support on the costs and outcomes of care for patients is difficult, though. At this stage, empirical research has shown that the use of health IT in general and CDS features in particular can improve the quality of patients' care, but it has not shown that improving care can, in turn, improve patients' health or reduce costs.

Several studies suggest that CDS features can improve the quality of health care:

- Garg and colleagues (2005) reviewed studies on clinical decision support and found that most such functions improved the performance of

---

[16] For example, the rate of back surgeries varies by state from just under 2 per 1,000 Medicare enrollees in Hawaii to more than 9 in Wyoming.

practitioners. Reminders about using established guidelines for preventive care were found to be the most effective feature. However, few of the studies that Garg reviewed also reported improved outcomes for patients.

- Asch and others (2004) found that the quality of care received by patients in the VA system, which uses an EHR that includes CDS tools, was superior to that received by a nationally representative sample of the population.[17] The VA practitioners' adherence to recommended-care guidelines was greatest for indicators of quality care that were associated with a VA performance measurement program (in which the care that practitioners provide is tracked and monitored and feedback is given to each practitioner about his or her performance). However, as CBO's 2008 report on geographic variation in health care spending notes, the VA medical system varies substantially across the nation in patterns of clinical practice, despite the fact that managers track providers' compliance with national guidelines for the treatment of many medical conditions.
- Consistent with the results from the VA, recently released data from a Medicare demonstration project of the Centers for Medicare and Medicaid Services (CMS) suggest that practitioners respond to rewards for high-quality care (Lindenauer and others, 2007). In that study, researchers coupled a CDS system with incentives to achieve a higher level of quality.

Yet a CDS capability does not always improve the quality of patients' care, and even if it could, that improvement might not have the desired effect on costs. According to a broad range of research (Crosson and others, 2007; Linder and others, 2007; Sequist and others, 2005; Tierney and others, 2005, 2003; Murray and others, 2004; Subramanian and others, 2004; Harris and others, 1998), CDS functions have failed to increase physicians' adherence to evidence-based standards of treatment for a wide variety of conditions, including chronic obstructive pulmonary disease, heart disease, diabetes, coronary artery disease, chronic heart failure, chronic renal insufficiency, and hypertension.

The failure to find positive effects from the use of CDS tools for those conditions could be due more to misaligned financial incentives than to

[17] Judged on the basis of 348 indicators used to assess the treatment of 26 conditions, best-practices care was provided for 67 percent of VA patients compared with 51 percent of non-VA patients. Particularly large differences between the two kinds of patients were seen in quality measurements of chronic disease care and preventive care.

limitations in the technology itself, or it could be attributable to the poor quality of some CDS features. Like all aspects of health IT, such tools are not uniform, nor are they all used equally well. The systems have been variously criticized as "cookbook" medicine, as not fitting well with the particular patterns of work in a given practice, or as unable to positively affect providers' behavior (Frisse, 2006; Sittig and others, 2006; Bates and others, 2003). With time, the quality of such systems may improve, and users may be better able to routinely achieve the positive effects noted in some studies.

Better CDS tools could also boost spending in some ways. For example, the use of some features (such as reminders to practitioners about screening tests and other preventive services) could increase spending for health care by encouraging the utilization of some additional services. Moreover, physicians might order some recommended preventive treatments that were not costeffective—because even though such practices might improve the health of patients, their costs might not be completely offset by reductions in future health care spending.

Generating Data for Research on Comparative Effectiveness and Cost-Effectiveness of Treatments. Proponents of the adoption of health IT note its potential to provide a massive source of new health care data—once patients' identifying information has been removed and the data have been standardized and assembled in a repository—for research on the comparative effectiveness and cost-effectiveness of medical treatments. The data could provide more-comprehensive information about the health histories of different patients and about the outcomes of their treatments than has previously been available. And the depth and breadth of the data would make it easier to take into account the differences among patients who receive different treatments and allow researchers to assess a broad set of outcomes.

Some work of that nature is being conducted through the HMO Research Network and through a broader network of centers having access to electronic databases that was established in 2005 by the Agency for Healthcare Research and Quality (Congressional Budget Office, 2007b). The knowledge gained from such studies could:

- Improve treatment protocols and methods,
- Lead to better outcomes for patients,
- Lower costs for health care
- Improve postmarketing surveillance of pharmaceuticals (to ensure that a drug is effective and has no unexpectedly harmful side effects) that have been approved by the Food and Drug Administration,
- Help target public health efforts, and

- Support early detection of outbreaks of diseases.

THE COSTS OF IMPLEMENTING HEALTH INFORMATION TECHNOLOGY

Implementing a health IT system, whether in a single physician's practice or in the multiple venues of an integrated health care delivery system, involves significant expenditures. Total costs for a health IT system include:

- The initial fixed cost of the hardware, software, and technical assistance necessary to install the system;
- Licensing fees;
- The expense of maintaining the system; and
- The "opportunity cost" of the time that health care providers could have spent seeing patients but instead must devote to learning how to use the new system and how to adjust their work practices accordingly.

The costs of implementing health IT systems vary widely among physicians and among hospitals, depending on the size and complexity of those providers' operations and the extent to which a system's users wish to perform their work electronically.

Owing in part to the wide variation in costs, evidence on expenditures for implementing health IT systems tends to be limited and somewhat conflicting. The initial investment and the cost of maintenance can be fairly easily determined—providers can obtain bids for a system from one or more vendors and thus have a relatively accurate estimate of what those costs will be once they have selected a vendor. Much less predictable is the productive time lost in learning to use the system and in adjusting patterns of work. Yet that nonmonetary investment may be an important factor in whether providers will be able to use the system effectively.

Social costs may also be a factor in providers' adoption and use of health IT, and one such potential cost is the risk of lost privacy. Purchasers of health IT systems, which must comply with stringent federal and state rules and standards intended to protect patients' privacy, bear the monetary costs associated with such protection. Given the ease with which information can be exchanged between health IT systems, patients whose physicians use them may feel that their privacy is more at risk than if paper records were used. (Health IT might also, though, support efforts to strengthen privacy by making it easier to track who accesses a patient's medical record.)

The Cost of Health IT Systems for Physicians' Offices

Estimating the total cost of implementing health IT systems in office-based medical practices is complicated by differences in the types and available features of the systems now being sold and differences in the characteristics of the practices that are adopting them. Many existing studies of the costs of implementing such systems lump together all direct costs (for hardware, software, licensing fees, installation, and training), do not include estimates of indirect costs (for example, practitioners' reduced productivity during the early stages of adoption), and spread the costs of implementation over different time frames.

The few detailed studies available report that total costs for office-based EHRs are about $25,000 to $45,000 per physician (Gans and others, 2005; Kibbe and Waldren, 2005).[18] Estimates of annual costs for operating and maintaining the system, which include software licensing fees, technical support, and updating and replacing used equipment, range between about 12 percent and 20 percent of initial costs, or $3,000 to $9,000 per physician per year (Miller and others, 2005; Wang and others, 2003).

Those studies indicate that smaller groups of physicians typically pay more per physician than do larger offices to implement health IT systems (Gans and others, 2005). Other possible savings may not depend on the size of a practice. Nearly all physicians already use information technology to manage the business side of their practices. Thus, many offices may already have much of the hardware necessary to operate a health IT system and need only purchase the software.

Moreover, the prices of health IT products appear to be falling (Kibbe and Waldren, 2005). In particular, some Internet-based applications that are becoming available might substantially limit costs to an annual subscription fee that could be as low as $2,000 per physician.[19] (However, extremely low prices might signal lower quality and fewer components or features.) If prices continue to fall over time, the quantity and quality of the health IT systems that are purchased should increase.

---

[18] The studies that CBO examined commonly report costs on a per- physician or per-hospital-bed basis. Some costs may vary in a given setting along those dimensions; others are more fixed.

[19] A list of those products and their prices as of September 2006 is available at www.physicianspractice.com/files/pdfs/theGuide_ sep06.pdf.

Physicians who implement health IT systems typically experience an initial loss in productivity as they learn how to use the system and adjust the ways in which they practice. In a survey of health IT adoption conducted by Gans and others (2005), many physicians' practices reported that after they implemented a system, productivity in their offices dropped by between 10 percent and 15 percent for at least several months. A study by Miller and colleagues (2005) found that among a sample of 14 small physicians' offices implementing a health IT system, the average drop in revenue from that loss of productivity was about $7,500 per physician. That amount may understate the actual loss in productivity, however, because in some practices, physicians worked longer hours to keep the practice's income the same as it was before the adoption.

The Cost of EHR and CPOE Systems for Hospitals

A few studies have examined the cost of implementing EHR and computerized physician order entry systems in hospitals.[20] Such calculations are difficult: Hospitals vary widely in size and type; a variety of different health IT applications may be implemented, and there is a general lack of data on costs. Those challenges limit the generalizability to other institutions of any single hospital's experience in implementing a health IT system.

For example, two studies—one in 2003 by First Consulting Group and the other reported in 2006 by Kaushal and colleagues—were carried out in teaching hospitals, making their results potentially unrepresentative of what would happen in a typical community hospital. First Consulting Group researchers used case studies of five hospitals or multihospital groups to develop a model for estimating hospitals' costs for adopting a CPOE system. According to that model, a large 500-bed hospital would incur initial costs of $7.9 million and annual operating costs of about $1.35 million; a smaller 250-bed hospital would incur initial costs of about $3 million and annual operating costs of approximately $700,000. On average, implementation costs for the health IT system amounted to about $14,500 per bed, and annual operating costs were about 19 percent of those one-time costs, or $2,700 per bed.

The study by the Kaushal research group considered the cost of implementing a CPOE system at Brigham and Women's Hospital, a 720-bed academic hospital in Boston affiliated with Harvard Medical School. That study reported costs

[20] EHR systems in hospitals generally include a CPOE component, so discussions of health IT in hospitals may use the two terms interchangeably.

totaling about $16,000 per year per bed for both implementation and maintenance between 1993 and 2002.

Researchers from the RAND Corporation (Girosi, Meili, and Scoville, 2005) estimated the costs of implementing CPOE systems using data from 27 teaching and nonacademic hospitals. That study reported a considerably higher average cost—nearly $63,000 per bed. The RAND researchers estimated that annual costs for maintaining and updating the system would equal 30 percent of acquisition costs—a figure that is higher than the corresponding proportion in other estimates and that adds $18,900 per bed per year. Although the RAND study used observations from a larger group of hospitals than the investigations discussed earlier, its sample was still quite small, and its estimates, as well as those of other researchers with small samples, should be viewed with caution.

Other factors may contribute to the variation in estimated costs for implementing hospitals' health IT systems. They include differences in the amounts and types of associated training and labor costs (for operating the system) that researchers may take into account and differences in the years from which the data are taken (because of changes from year to year in the technologies, in costs, and in other factors). The RAND analysts observed a relatively linear relationship between the number of beds in a hospital and the hospital's costs for implementing a health IT system and posited that health IT costs were budget driven; that is, such costs are influenced by the amount of money that the hospital has allocated for spending on health IT in general, and various projects, including an EHR or CPOE system, are funded as they rise to the top of the hospitals' list of priorities. Budgets for information technology for hospitals typically range from 1 percent to 3 percent of overall operating expenses. Hospitals that are part of integrated delivery systems with very sophisticated clinical IT capabilities (including those in outpatient settings) may have budgets for information technology that equal or exceed 4 percent.[21]

Possible Factors to Explain the Low Rates of Adoption of Health IT

In spite of the seeming advantages that health IT offers to physicians and hospitals, the proportion of those providers that actually use such systems is

[21] Personal communications to CBO staff from James Walker, Chief Information Officer, Geisinger Health System, May 19, 2008; and Len Bowes, Senior Medical Informaticist, Intermountain Healthcare, May 18, 2008.

relatively small. Several factors may explain the low rate of adoption, including the challenges that arise in implementing the systems, the inability of providers to capture all of the financial returns of the health IT systems that they purchase, the possibility in the case of health insurance plans that the efficiencies they garner through the use of health IT will benefit their competitors, and uncertainty about the value of the advantages to be gained from adopting a health IT system and the evolution of laws affecting its acquisition and financing.

Challenges in Implementing Health IT Systems

Adopting a health IT system involves more than just deciding to spend money; it is a major organizational commitment that, for hospitals in particular, will probably last for several years. To take full advantage of such a system may require physicians to substantially redesign the way they practice medicine. EHRs are only as helpful as the information that goes into them. Some of that information is part of the system when it is purchased, but much of the technology's value comes when physicians devote considerable time to training, to personalizing the system, and to adapting their work processes to achieve the maximum benefits. Not surprisingly, the adoption rates for health IT systems are higher among younger physicians, who in general are more familiar with computers than their older colleagues (who were trained with paper charts as an integral part of patients' care and who may be more comfortable using such tools in their practices; Grossman and Reed, 2006).

In implementing a health IT system, providers must choose from among a wide array of vendors and options. With so many choices (for example, more than 40 different EMR vendors) and rapidly developing technologies, many providers may be concerned about buying the wrong kind of system for their practice, acquiring technology that has already become outdated, or purchasing a poor-quality system. They may wish to postpone the decision until more of their colleagues have purchased systems, allowing them to benefit from others' experience. Research suggests that providers who have purchased an EHR system tend to be in practices in which at least one physician is technically savvy and able to champion the cause of health IT (Miller and Sim, 2004). But relatively few practices include such a physician, which may lead many providers to wait until the systems become more standardized and demand coalesces around fewer but better-known choices. The large number of vendors and products may slow down adoption in the short run, but the winnowing process that occurs as some vendors leave the market is likely to identify the products that deliver the greatest value per dollar spent.

As noted earlier, the prices of health IT systems are falling, and over time that decline should lead to an increase in purchases. One question is whether such increased demand would be constrained by supply problems for qualified technicians to install and maintain the systems. Indeed, hospitals and large provider groups have already begun to complain about the difficulty of finding qualified technicians to maintain their systems.

Providers' Inability to Capture Financial Returns from Health IT

Many, if not most, providers would like to make more use of health IT in their practices, recognizing the technology's potential to improve the quality of the care they provide, increase convenience for their patients, and perhaps reduce costs in their office. But many of those benefits accrue to others rather than to the providers who purchase the health IT system As a result, many providers cannot generate the additional income necessary to justify the significant investment in time and money that the adoption of such a system would require.

Some benefits to be derived from health IT increase in value as the network of those using the technology expands—that is, as other providers also purchase health IT systems. Providers who can perform functions electronically (such as communicating with each other, sending and receiving medical records, prescribing medications electronically, and ordering laboratory and imaging procedures) gain when other providers develop similar electronic capabilities. For example, the cost to a primary care physician of sending medical data to a consulting specialist is far lower with a health IT system—as long as the consulting specialist has an interoperable system that can receive the data electronically. However, some so- called network benefits accrue mainly to patients or health insurance plans and only indirectly to providers. Examples include less duplication of diagnostic tests or increased availability of patient data in accessible repositories, which could lead to more research on the best practices for treatment and care.

Health IT can contribute to improvements in the quality of health care that providers deliver, but it is relatively rare for providers to be compensated for such improvements. Pay-for-performance programs are in effect in some managed care plans in the Medicaid program and as pilot programs in the fee-for-service sector of Medicare. Such programs do not create a strong incentive to invest in health IT systems, though, because the payments are fairly modest. Another approach that

Medicare has adopted is to not pay for poor performance in some areas. CMS recently began a program under which it will not pay for certain occurrences that it calls "never events" or "serious preventable events" (Department of Health and Human Services, 2008). Never events include such incidents as leaving an object in a patient's body during a surgery; operating on the wrong patient or on the wrong body part of the right patient, or performing the wrong surgery; precipitating an air embolism as a result of surgery (in general, an air embolism is a bubble of air in a blood vessel that may cause trouble if it moves to the heart or brain); and providing incompatible blood or blood products. Never events occur rarely, and not paying for a service that leads to such an event is unlikely to have a big effect on providers' behavior in adopting health IT.

Other than through such programs, the financial rewards for physicians and hospitals from improving the quality of their care (or avoiding the provision of poor-quality services) are indirect. A physician's reputation for providing high-quality care might improve as a result of investing in health IT, and patients might want to see a physician who uses an EHR because they believe they will get better-quality care. Health plans, in recruiting doctors for their networks of physicians, might eventually find that doctors who used health IT systems were more attractive to patients than physicians who did not—provided that the plans could determine whether those doctors actually helped them attract and retain enrollees or lowered the cost of treating them.

Most networks of physicians today, however, cover nearly all the doctors in a given area, so physicians who were considering an investment in health IT would probably not include in their calculations whether their use of the technology would make their services more attractive to health insurers. They would also probably not expect to increase their income by improving the quality of the care they provided; thus, that factor would probably not be a key consideration for them. However, they might change their thinking if they knew that they would be directly compensated for implementing a health IT system or if they could report data on the quality of care that they provided—data for which they were being compensated—only by using such a system.

Other benefits, such as lower costs for maintaining medical records and transcribing clinical data, clearly accrue to the provider who purchases the health IT system. For example, Intermountain Healthcare reports that its savings from reducing transcription costs alone (as high as $12,500 per year for some physicians) contributed substantially to paying for its EHR, which cost about

$2,500 per physician.[22] But many providers, especially primary care physicians in small practices, might gain relatively little from implementing such a system because their practice would be too small to benefit from the efficiencies it would create. (For example, many providers would not save on transcription costs by purchasing a health IT system because they were not using transcription to begin with).

Competition among Health Insurance Plans

Health insurance companies may have an incentive to help providers acquire health IT systems: The technology could help lower the companies' costs by improving both the quality of the care that providers deliver and patients' health. But competition may limit the amount of assistance insurers give to providers to implement health IT systems because the same savings and improvements in quality that such a payer might reap if providers used a health IT system could also benefit competing health insurance plans.

For example, suppose Plan A paid an additional amount per unit of service to providers who used EHRs in their offices. That additional payment would probably be determined by the benefit per patient that the plan expected to receive from the physician's use of the system (a benefit that the physician could not capture). But Plan A could not realize all of that benefit, either because some of it would go to other payers—for example, Plan B, a competitor of Plan A, whose participants were seen by the same physician. If Plan B contracted with the same physicians that Plan A used but made no additional payment for the adoption of health IT, it would obtain the same benefit that Plan A obtained from improved quality and lower costs but would not have to pay for it. Thus, even though payers might gain many of the benefits that providers are unable to garner, a payer's inability to prevent competitors from also gaining those benefits may limit the assistance it is willing to give providers to obtain the technology.

Health insurance plans might also hesitate to help pay for the adoption of health IT systems by providers because they cannot fully capture the returns from improving the quality of health care services that such systems may bring. Health plans undergo open enrollment each year, and many enrollees switch from one plan to another during that time. Unless the improved quality of care yielded savings quickly, it would probably do little to motivate insurers to help providers

---

[22] Personal communication to CBO from Len Bowes, Senior Medical Informaticist, Intermountain Healthcare, May 18, 2008; Clayton and others (2005).

adopt health IT. In fact, health care plans largely address the quality of health care services only to the extent that the employers who purchase coverage for their employees demand it. Many employers are beginning to ask plans to take steps to improve the quality of health care. However, even very large employers may have little leverage with insurance companies to encourage improvements because their workers are usually dispersed across the country. And few employers have enough employees in any one community to enable them to demand changes. In addition, the outcomes for people's health that improvements in the quality of care might provide are still unknown in many cases because not enough research has been done.

Rather than help providers obtain EHRs for their offices, some insurers use other types of electronic records, such as personal health records (PHRs) and payer-based health records (PBHRs). The PHR is controlled by the patient, the PBHR by the health insurance plan (see the appendix for additional information). Both types of electronic record deliver at least some of the network benefits to payers that would be available if physicians used health IT systems, and they present fewer issues related to competition. For example, even though the information in PBRs and PBHRs is not at the same level of detail as the data in EHRs, such records could still help eliminate duplicate diagnostic tests and identify current medications and medical conditions through the data on insurance claims that they do include—information that would be helpful, for example, in a hospital emergency room. But even these alternatives to EHRs have encountered obstacles to implementation related to competition. Payers in some markets have been reluctant to share claims data and other information, fearing that competitors could use it to their detriment.

Worries that the use of health IT will benefit competitors are not limited to health plans. Hospitals and other providers may be concerned that such systems will cause them to lose some degree of control over what they may consider to be proprietary information: the information in their patients' charts. Patients always have the right to access their medical records, but if the records are paper, the impediments to doing so (including the need to make copies) naturally limit the number and nature of the inquiries they are likely to make. Medical data that are stored electronically, however, coupled with the growing availability and popularity of personal health records, imply less control of health data by providers and more control by patients—and potentially greater access to those records by other providers and health plans.

The increased availability of that information through the use of EHRs improves the quality of care for patients. (For example, a hospital emergency room with access to a patient's primary care physician's medical record can better treat that patient, and researchers have more data for evaluating the effectiveness of various medical treatments.) But some providers could lose patients to competitors; the fact that electronic medical records can be so easily transferred makes it easier for patients to change physicians. Providers might also worry that the ease of documentation and emphasis on greater transparency could have a negative impact if it showed them to be less competent than other competing providers.

Box 2. The Federal Government's Activities as a Payer

The federal government can influence the development and growth of health information technology (health IT) through its operation and management of federal programs that finance health care—in particular, Medicare, which accounts for about 20 percent of all third-party (insurance) payments in the United States, and Medicaid, a joint program with the states for which the federal government's share of spending accounts for 8 percent of third-party payments. In addition to those two programs, the federal government pays for or provides health care through the Military Health System, the Veterans Health Administration, the Indian Health Service, and the Federal Employees Health Benefits Program.

What exactly the government should require of health care providers in those programs is beyond the scope of this paper. It is reasonable, however, to expect that the government would ask the same questions asked by private health insurance plans about the costs versus benefits of various health IT systems and that it would either encourage or require participating providers to use systems that are consistent with sound management of federally managed or funded health care programs. Because the government is not concerned about competitive issues, its efforts with regard to health IT are not constrained by fears of benefiting health insurance plans in the private sector.

The Centers for Medicare and Medicaid Services (CMS), which runs Medicare, has undertaken a number of initiatives and programs that encourage the adoption of health IT:

- The Medicare Care Management Demonstration provides financial incentives to medical practices on the basis of their performance on 26 measures of clinical quality. Physicians who use an electronic health record (EHR) certified by the Certification Commission for Healthcare Information Technology and who submit performance data to CMS electronically receive additional payments.
- In another demonstration announced in October 2007, CMS will make

bonus payments to small physician practices that use certified EHRs. All participating practices will be required to use a certified EHR to perform specific functions, such as clinical documentation and electronic ordering of prescriptions (e-prescribing), that can positively affect the quality of patients' care. The core incentive payment to the practices will be based on their performance on measures of quality, with an enhanced bonus based on how well integrated the EHR is in helping physicians manage care.

- In accordance with a recently passed law, CMS is implementing the Physicians Quality Reporting Initiative, through which physicians receive extra compensation for submitting data to CMS on the quality of the care they deliver. (Although physicians are not required to use health IT systems to prepare and transmit those reports, such systems facilitate that reporting.)
- CMS is working with Medicare Advantage plans, the program's managed care option, to encourage them to offer personal health records (described in the appendix) to their members.
- CMS published a rule in 2006 and recently proposed another that would establish standards for e-prescribing for the Medicare program. The rules do not require providers to use e-prescribing in their practices; however, if providers are planning to use such an application to prescribe medication for their Medicare patients, they must abide by the CMS standards.

In addition to creating payment incentives to encourage providers to adopt health IT, CMS is working— as are a number of private health insurance plans—to develop policies for the use of health IT and standards for the systems. For example, CMS is a member of the American Health Information Community (a federal advisory committee established by the Department of Health and Human Services, or HHS) and participates in many of its working groups. In 2007, CMS administered a total of $98 million in grants to states for the Medicaid Transformation program; the bulk of those grants were focused on implementing e-prescribing, EHRs, and the capability for health information exchange. CMS also provides technical assistance to small and medium-sized physician practices to help them obtain health IT systems and coaching for practices that acquire health IT practice management systems.

Other federal agencies that purchase health care are also involved in efforts to further the development and broad adoption of health IT. The Department of Defense (DoD), the Department of Veterans Affairs (VA), and the Office of Personnel Management (OPM) have worked with HHS to adopt health information standards for use by all federal health agencies. As part of the Consolidated Health Informatics initiative, more than 20 federal agencies have agreed to endorse standards that enable information to be shared among agencies and that can serve as a model for the private sector. OPM has agreed to create incentives aimed at encouraging providers to adopt health IT in its contracts with insurers that participate in the Federal Employees Health Benefits Program.

The VA and DoD are both extensive users of health IT. For several years, the VA has used an EHR, the Veterans Health Information Systems and Technology Architecture (VistA), in providing care to U.S. military veterans and, according to some empirical studies, has improved the efficiency of its health care delivery and the quality of the care it provides. The VA has made VistA an "open source" system—available to the public at no charge—thereby lessening the cost to providers of adopting health IT.[1] DoD has developed and is in the process of implementing an EHR—known as AHLTA [armed forces health longitudinal technology application]—for its health care system. Currently, AHLTA gives health care providers access to data about the conditions that beneficiaries are being treated for and their prescriptions and diagnostic tests, as well as additional information. DoD is also working with the VA to develop a way by which health information can be transmitted seamlessly and instantaneously between the two agencies.

***

1. The open-source version of VistA is known as WorldVistA. Although it is free, it is a relatively sophisticated system that may be intimidating for providers who have little experience with computers. An additional drawback for such providers is that WorldVistA may not come with the same level of on- call technical support and other similar types of assistancethat are typically part of the EHR products of for-profit vendors.

The perceived loss of control of health data that makes some providers reluctant to adopt health IT may also make them hesitate to share information if they implement EHRs in their practice. Such reluctance has been a major stumbling block in efforts to establish and maintain regional health information organizations and to support greater exchange of health care information.[23]

Regulatory Impediments

State and federal regulations regarding health IT are evolving. One major issue concerns federal rules related to donations of health IT that hospitals and

[23] More information on the challenges in establishing regional health information is available at www.ehealthinitiative.org/toolkit/ alifin/VSMFiles/HRSA_CCBH_Report_Summary.pdf

other large providers may want to make to providers with whom they work. Recent changes in such rules have created so- called safe harbors that allow those donations to take place without violating prohibitions on physician self- referrals. But some providers, payers, and other participants in the health care sector may be reluctant to make or accept donations until the rules regarding them are clearer.

The Departments of Health and Human Services (HHS) and Justice have attempted to clarify those rules, but other agencies, including the Internal Revenue Service (IRS), are still developing their regulations. The IRS has addressed the question of nonprofit hospitals' donations of health IT to physicians, but it is still studying related issues, such as the tax-exempt status of regional health information organizations and of organizations formed by payers and others to promote the adoption of health IT.

A major aspect of policymaking in regard to health IT has to do with ensuring that proper safeguards are in place to protect confidentiality and patients' privacy. The ability of health IT systems to speed the exchange of data and expand the amount of information that is shared also increases the risk that the confidentiality of personal health care information could be compromised (although in one sense EMR and other systems could lessen that risk by making it easier to monitor who accesses a person's medical record). Efforts to clarify and update federal and state laws regarding privacy are well under way, but the final form of those laws is uncertain—another factor that could be constraining the widespread adoption of health IT.

THE FEDERAL ROLE IN IMPLEMENTING HEALTH INFORMATION TECHNOLOGY

The federal government is both a purchaser of health care services and a regulator of health IT. As a purchaser, the government has an interest in improving the quality and the value of the care provided by Medicare, Medicaid, and other federal health care programs (which together account for about one-third of total national expenditures on health care). If, indeed, health IT improves the quality of care while lowering its costs, then the federal government as a payer might consider actions that would facilitate the adoption of health IT, as long as the costs of those actions did not exceed the savings expected from them or the value of the improvements in care. (Box 2 on page 22 describes federal activities relating to the government's role as a purchaser of health care services)

As a regulator, the government is helping coordinate and facilitate the development and use of health IT. In general, its regulatory actions have been limited to functions (such as developing standards for interoperability) that would appear to be more difficult, more time-consuming, or more costly than those that the private sector could deal with on its own. (Box 3 describes federal activities relating to the government's role as a regulator).

Box 3. The Federal Government's Activities as a Regulator and Funder

The Department of Health and Human Services (HHS), through the Office of the National Coordinator for Health Information Technology (ONC), leads the federal government's efforts to encourage the adoption of health information technology (health IT). ONC's primary responsibilities are to coordinate the development of standards for health IT systems to ensure interoperability (the systems' capability to communicate with each other) and the development and implementation of a national health information network through which inter- operable health information can be exchanged. (For additional information, see Box 1 on page 2.)

To help spur adoption of health IT, HHS has established a new rule—which was developed by the Centers for Medicare and Medicaid Services and the HHS inspector general—to make it easier for hospitals and other entities to give health IT systems to physicians. (The incentive for a hospital to provide health IT equipment and technical assistance to physicians who are associated with it is that such inter- operable health IT systems may enable the hospital to better control its costs and improve the quality of the care it provides.) The new rule creates two new exceptions to a so-called physician "self-referral" law, which prohibits a physician—unless an exception applies—from referring Medicare patients for certain designated health services to entities with which the physician has a financial relationship. The two new exceptions are as follows: First, entities that furnish the designated health services may give to physicians interoperable electronic health record (EHR) software, information technology, and training services; and second, hospitals and other entities may provide physicians with hardware, software, or other information technology and training necessary and used solely for the electronic prescribing of medications. The rule also specifies that recipients of such health IT donations pay at least 15 percent of the price of the system.

HHS has also supported the development of health IT through grants administered by ONC and the activities of other HHS agencies. The department has funded efforts to enhance the privacy and security of personal health information, promote antifraud activities for EHRs, support the development of standardized measures of adoption for such records, and organize groups of qualified experts to advise the federal government in its activities concerning the clinical decision support feature of many EHRs.

The Agency for Healthcare Research and Quality within HHS funds research and development to support and stimulate investment in health IT, especially in rural and underserved areas. The agency also created the National Resource Center for Health Information Technology, which provides technical assistance on health IT. The Health Resources and Services Administration within HHS provides technical assistance as well to health centers and other grantees in adopting model practices and technologies.

HHS has also provided funds to other entities. In 2005, it established the American Health Information Community (AHIC), a federal advisory committee made up of public- and private-sector leaders who represent a broad spectrum of health care stakeholders. AHIC was established to make recommendations to the Secretary of Health and Human Services on how to make health records digital and interoperable and ensure that the privacy and security of the records are protected; it is charged with accomplishing those goals by relying as much as possible on the private sector. (Other private-sector entities established with the assistance of HHS funding include the Health Information Technology Standards Panel and the Certification Commission for Healthcare Information Technology; see Box 1 for additional information)

Issues for Consideration

As the prominence of health IT has grown—in terms of its potential for increasing the efficiency and improving the quality of health care—policymakers have debated the appropriateness of the federal government's being involved in stimulating and guiding its adoption. Two factors lend support for such a role. The first is the federal government's position as a major purchaser of health care services through such programs as Medicare and Medicaid. As the manager of those programs, the government is responsible for running them efficiently and maintaining a level of quality in their services that reflects the views of the electorate as expressed by policymakers. As a payer, the federal government assesses the benefits and costs of health IT in its various forms, determines which elements of the technology should be required to run federal health care financing programs efficiently and at the desired level of quality, and takes appropriate steps to achieve the level of use of health IT that meets those criteria.

The second factor lending support to possible federal intervention in furthering adoption of health IT is that the technology has some characteristics of a public good—that is, a good that would be provided in a lessthan-optimal amount by private markets if the government did not intervene. A fundamental characteristic of a public good is the presence of a free-rider problem, whereby some of the parties that directly benefit from the good are able to secure its advantages without being charged for them. Such goods are undersupplied because the receipts that they generate for their producers do not adequately represent their value to individuals (because consumers of the good can obtain its benefits without paying for them).

One feature of health IT that may qualify as a public good is the wealth of information that can be captured through EHR systems. (As discussed earlier, if researchers combined data from the EHRs of the population, they might be able to understand the spread and prevention of various diseases and injuries—and eventually develop cures and treatments; assess the effectiveness of various treatments; and more readily detect potential treatment hazards.) Some analysts contend that because such information is a public good—once generated, it would not be feasible to restrict its use—it is unlikely to be produced without the government's intervention. According to that argument, the government has an interest in the adoption of health IT systems that could readily generate such data and therefore a reason to become involved in standardizing coding systems and methods. In addition, the government would want to encourage the recording of such information and subsequent analytical studies as well as the dissemination of results.

Health IT also resembles a public good because of its network effects: Some of its benefits increase in value as more providers purchase and use interoperable systems. Those benefits include, for example, being able to exchange relevant medical information electronically, a less expensive option than the use of paper. The additional user of health IT provides a benefit to existing users in the community that is available to all of them at little or no additional cost and from which it is difficult to exclude an existing user. Because a would-be purchaser of health IT fails to account for the value of the network's expansion in calculating the benefits to be gained from implementing such a system, too few people (relative to the number that would enhance overall economic wellbeing to the greatest degree) will purchase health IT systems.

Given that the returns of health IT to the providers who invest in such systems are less than the returns to society as a whole, an argument could be made that the federal government's intervention is necessary to raise the rate of the technology's adoption to be more in line with its total returns. But the fact that health IT has some characteristics of a public good does not necessarily mean that the federal government must intervene, nor does it prescribe an appropriate form of intervention. Another alternative for enhancing adoption might be private-sector cooperative arrangements to help providers purchase systems that would be jointly funded by the participants and that would benefit the market as a whole. Some areas of the country, such as Indiana, boast successful regional health information organizations that, without federal assistance, facilitate the broad exchange of health care information within a community. Similarly, markets for products that have networklike benefits have developed in other cases without the government's help. The market for fax machines, a product that provides network benefits, is an example.

Relying on private markets to act, however, would probably lead to a slower rate of adoption than if the federal government intervened. Private-sector participants would have to engage in time-consuming negotiations to reach agreements acceptable to most parties. By contrast, the government could either limit its intervention to such activities as setting standards and supporting the development of regional networks for health information exchange or act more broadly to encourage health care providers and payers to purchase health IT systems.

The government may also have a special interest in protecting individuals' rights with respect to health information, especially in regard to privacy and people's access to personal health records. Competing interests are involved in relation to privacy issues. On the one hand, people expect and hope that their individual privacy will be protected in electronic transactions regarding their health care. On the other hand, researchers seeking to improve health care outcomes would like relatively free access to health care data for use in their work. Many analysts believe that given those competing interests, the government's involvement is critical in developing rules to protect individuals' privacy in health care transactions but still facilitate relatively unfettered access to personal health records for the purposes of research.

Options for Federal Efforts to Promote Adoption of Health IT

If the federal government chose to intervene directly to promote the use of health IT, it could do so by subsidizing that use or by requiring it. Steps might include, for example, having Medicare pay an additional amount per billed service to providers who used EHRs or requiring that providers who wished to participate in Medicare obtain an EHR by a specified date or pay a penalty. From a budgetary perspective, the subsidization approach is less likely to generate cost savings for the federal government because of the direct budgetary costs of the subsidy.

Paying a bonus to providers that used health IT (in an amount less than or equal to the value of the providers' use of the technologies) would enable practitioners to capture more of the benefits that their use of health IT would produce and give them a stronger financial incentive to invest in a system. But that approach would be likely to lead to a net cost for the government—and possibly a large one. Even a small bonus could be expensive because it would be paid not only to those providers who newly purchased health IT but also to providers who already had such systems. Because a small bonus would attract relatively few takers, the bulk of the bonus would be paid to providers that already had health IT. A large bonus would entice more new purchasers, but it would add further to the overall net cost of the federal subsidy. (An alternative approach might be to target a subsidy to various types of providers, the amount of which would depend on their ability to capture the financial benefits of health IT. Thus, providers who were associated with staff- model HMOs and other highly integrated organizations would receive relatively small subsidies, whereas solo providers would receive relatively larger amounts)

A mandate to purchase health IT, or to purchase a particular functionality such as e-prescribing, by contrast, would probably induce nearly all providers to adopt it at a small cost to the government, and might produce net savings in health care spending. The requirement could be enforced either by not paying providers who failed to adopt such a system for other health care services that they delivered, or by imposing a specific penalty on those who did not comply. A less prescriptive version would involve paying providers without a health IT system less for any given procedure than providers with a health IT system were paid, which would create an implicit penalty for failing to adopt the technology. Either of those approaches, though, would come at a cost to providers, and that cost would be greatest for providers who were least able to capture the financial benefits of health IT systems. If policymakers are interested in promoting health IT, some version of a requirement or an explicit or implicit penalty for providers who fail to adopt health IT is likely to be more cost-effective for the federal government than a subsidy.

APPENDIX: COMMON TERMS IN HEALTH INFORMATION TECHNOLOGY

Health information technology (health IT) is a broad term that is commonly used to describe the use of computers and electronic applications in providing and documenting medical care. The most common health IT terms include several types of health records—the electronic medical record (EMR), the electronic health record (EHR), and the patient health record (PHR)—as well as computerized physician order entry (CPOE), clinical decision support (CDS), electronic prescribing (e- prescribing), and interoperability. EMRs, particularly those in hospitals, in many cases include CPOE and CDS applications. Also part of the health IT landscape are the health information exchanges (HIEs) and regional health information organizations (RHIOs)[24]

The electronic medical record is equivalent to the paper- based medical record that a health care provider maintains for a patient. The National Alliance for Health Information Technology defines it as "[a] computer- accessible resource of medical and administrative information available on an individual collected from and accessible by providers involved in the individual's care within a single care setting." The EMR contains demographic information and clinical data (related to the practice of medicine) on the individual, including information about medications, the patient's medical history, and the doctor's clinical notes (Moshman Associates, Inc., and Booz Allen Hamilton, 2006). The EMRs currently in use vary considerably. Basic systems include patient information, doctors' clinical notes, and results from diagnostic tests. Systems that are more sophisticated also include such features as e-prescribing and warnings about drug and allergy interactions. The most advanced EMRs add CPOE (see below), registry functions that support population management, and clinical decision support.[25] The variation in what different EMRs can provide has complicated measurements of the rate of their adoption and led to seemingly contradictory estimates.

---

[24] The definitions included here draw heavily on an interim draft document prepared by the National Alliance for Health Information Technology, with guidance from BearingPoint, Inc. The effort is funded by the Office of the National Coordinator for Health Information Technology to achieve consensus on definitions for five health IT terms: electronic health record, electronic medical record, personal health record, regional health information organization, and health information exchange.

[25] Registries generally track patients who have a particular disease or who have received a specific treatment. They collect additional information (such as measures of health status or test results) that is typically not contained in insurance claims records.

An *electronic health record* is defined as "[a] computer- accessible, interoperable [see below] resource of clinical and administrative information pertinent to the health of an individual." An EHR differs from an EMR in that information is drawn from multiple clinical and administrative sources and used primarily by a broad spectrum of clinical personnel involved in the individual's care, enabling them to deliver and coordinate care and promote the person's wellness. Any ambulatory-care EMR that meets the certification requirements of the Certification Commission for Healthcare Information Technology (see Box 1 on page 2 for more information) and that includes access to data sources beyond the physician's office would be termed an electronic health record with the EMR embedded in it. Despite their differences, the terms "EMR" and "EHR" are often used interchangeably.

A *personal health record* is another type of electronic record that is distinguished in part by who controls it: A PHR is controlled by the patient, whereas the EHR is controlled by the provider. The PHR is defined as "[a] computer-accessible, interoperable [see below] resource of pertinent health information on an individual. Individuals manage and determine the rights to the access, use, and control of the information. The information originates from multiple sources and is used by individuals and their authorized clinical and wellness professionals to help guide and make health decisions." In contrast to the EHR, in which providers enter data, people who use a PHR manage the data contained in it. As a result, the quality and comprehensiveness of the information in a PHR vary considerably, depending on how much effort the patient wishes to expend and his or her access to data.

PHRs may and frequently do include data on insurance claims for medical services that the patient has received. (Some health insurance plans now provide PHRs to their members and insert their claims data.) By comparison, EHRs typically contain data that are more clinical in nature, such as the physician's notes on treatment or services provided. (They may also contain data from other providers if the patient was referred to a specialist.) In essence, the PHR's data are broad but not especially deep, whereas the EHR's data are less broad but much deeper. The PHR, however, has the potential to be the basis for the electronic health record, the repository for all health data on a particular patient.

Many health plans and some employers now offer the use of PHRs to their members or employees, but while such a record can be a benefit to consumers, it may also raise questions about who owns the record, how it can be used, and whether the data in the record can be transferred if the person switches health plans or employers. Firms such as Google and Microsoft are now (or soon will be) offering a PHR product.

A *payer-based health* record (PBHR), yet another type of electronic health record, is owned and administered by a health plan. It includes whatever data are available to the health plan but primarily those related to claims. It may also include demographic information provided by the patient at the time of enrollment. It does not contain clinical notes; however, owing to the increasing amount of data required in submitting claims to payers, a PBHR may comprise laboratory results, radiological readings, prescriptions, and complete reports for inpatient and outpatient hospital care, as well as other types of information. A PBHR may be useful—for example, when a patient visits a hospital emergency room—because hospital staff can access the record to obtain critical data on the patient, such as information that could help prevent adverse drug events.

Computerized physician order entry systems are electronic applications that physicians use to order medications, diagnostic (laboratory and radiology) tests, and ancillary services (Poon and others, 2004). Typically, such systems are used in hospitals, often with an EHR; however, many outpatient EHRs also provide CPOE functions. Because EHRs and CPOE are so often connected in hospitals, a facility's health IT system may be described as either an EMR, an EHR, or a CPOE system, adding to the confusion over what system the hospital is actually using. (Studies that examine the effects of health IT in hospitals often measure reductions in duplicate orders for laboratory tests, and those reductions are possible only if the hospital has both an EHR and a CPOE system).

Clinical decision support systems are often used in combination with CPOE functions in hospitals to assist physicians with decisionmaking by providing reminders, suggestions, and support in diagnosing and treating diseases and conditions. The range of features that CDS systems offer includes drug-dosing assistance, checks for drug allergies and drug-drug interactions, access to the latest evidence-based protocols, reminders about preventive- medicine tests, and guidance for complex antibiotic management programs. Both CPOE and CDS systems vary considerably in their complexity and capabilities.

E-prescribing is the electronic transfer of a prescription from the prescribing physician's office to the pharmacy, which allows a patient to make only a single trip to the pharmacy to pick up the prescription once it has been filled. E-prescribing has received a great deal of attention but is not very common. Many physicians who have EHRs in place could easily generate prescriptions using the electronic record—and thus benefit from the CDS function that many EHRs include—but in the end they often print out a prescription for the patient to take to the pharmacy. Using the EHR to generate a paper prescription may reduce transcription errors and reduce the physician's time and effort, but the patient must still deliver the prescription to the pharmacy.

Interoperability describes the capacity of one health IT application to share information with another in a computable format (that is, for example, not simply by sharing a PDF [portable document format] file). Sharing information within and across health IT tools depends on the use of a standardized format for communicating information electronically—both among the components that constitute a doctor's office EHR (clinical notes, lab results, and radiological imaging and results) and among providers and settings that use different health IT applications. An interoperable health IT system would allow a hospital physician to view the contents of an EHR from a patient's primary care physician and enable the primary care physician in turn to view all notes and diagnostic tests from the patient's hospital visit. Interoperability is the feature that would allow the creation of a single comprehensive medical record that could follow a person throughout his or her life and from one geographic area to another.

A key component of interoperability is the establishment of a health information exchange, an "information highway" of sorts. An HIE is defined as "the electronic movement of any and all health-related data according to an agreed-upon set of interoperability standards, processes and activities across nonaffiliated organizations in a manner that protects the privacy and security of that data; and the entity that organizes and takes responsibility for the process." Without such an arrangement, a physician could still receive lab results in a computable format and use e-prescribing, but a hospital could not, for example, access information on a patient that is stored in the physician's office EHR. Health information exchanges are even less common than EHRs; however, some integrated health care delivery systems, such as Intermountain Healthcare in Utah and southern Idaho and the Veterans Health Administration, share information within their networks and operate much like health information exchanges. However, because they have access only to data within the network, they may not have a comprehensive view of a patient's record.

A *regional health* information organization is defined as "a multi-stakeholder governance entity that convenes nonaffiliated health and healthcare-related providers and the beneficiaries they serve, for the purpose of improving health care for the communities in which it operates. It takes responsibility for the processes that enable the electronic exchange of interoperable health information within a defined contiguous geographic area."

REFERENCES

American Hospital Association. 2007. *Continued Progress: Hospital Use of Information Technology*. Chicago, Ill.: American Hospital Association. Available at www.aha.org/aha/content/2007/pdf/070227-continued progress.pdf.

Anderson, Gerard F., and others. 2006. "Health Care Spending and Use of Information Technology in OECD Countries." *Health Affairs*, vol. 25, no. 3 (May–June), pp. 819–831.

Asch, Steven M., and others. 2004. "Comparison of Quality of Care for Patients in the Veterans Health Administration and Patients in a National Sample." *Annals of Internal Medicine*, vol. 141, no. 12 (December 21), pp. 938–945.

Baker, Laurence C. 2005. "Benefits of Interoperability: A Closer Look at the Estimates." *Health Affairs*, Web Exclusive (January 19), pp. w5-22–25.

Bates, David W., and others. 2003. "Ten Commandments for Effective Clinical Decision Support: Making the Practice of Evidence-Based Medicine a Reality." *Journal of the American Medical Informatics Association*, vol. 10, no. 6 (November–December), pp. 523–530.

Bates, David W., and others. 1999a. "The Impact of Computerized Physician Order Entry on Medication Error Prevention." *Journal of the American Medical Informatics Association*, vol. 6, no. 4 (July–August), pp. 313—321.

Bates, David W., and others. 1999b. "A Randomized Trial of a Computer-Based Intervention to Reduce Utilization of Redundant Laboratory Tests." *American Journal of Medicine*, vol. 106, no. 2 (February), pp. 144–150.

Bates, David W., and others. 1998a. "Effect of Computerized Physician Order Entry and a Team Intervention on Prevention of Serious Medication Errors." *Journal of the American Medical Association*, vol. 280, no. 15 (October 21), pp. 1311–1316.

Bates, David W., and others. 1 998b. "What Proportion of Common Diagnostic Tests Appear Redundant?" *American Journal of Medicine*, vol. 104, no. 4 (April), pp. 361–368.

Clayton, Paul D., and others. 2005. "Physician Use of Electronic Medical Records: Issues and Successes with Direct Data Entry and Physician Productivity." *American Medical Informatics Association Annual Symposium Proceedings,* pp. 141–145.

Congressional Budget Office. 2008. Geographic Variation in Health Care Spending. Available at www.cbo.gov/ ftpdocs/89xx/doc8972/02-15-GeogHealth.pdf.

Congressional Budget Office. 2007a. *The Health Care System for Veterans: An Interim Report.* Available at www.cbo.gov/ftpdocs/88xx/doc8892/12-21-VA_Healthcare.pdf.

Congressional Budget Office. 2007b. *Research on the Comparative Effectiveness of Medical Treatments:Issues and Options for an Expanded Federal Role.* Available at www.cbo.gov/ftpdocs/88xx/doc8891/12-18-ComparativeEffectiveness.pdf.

Crosson, Jesse C., and others. 2007. "Electronic Medical Records and Diabetes Quality of Care: Results from a Sample of Family Medicine Practices." *Annals of Family Medicine*, vol. 5, no. 3 (May–June), pp. 209–215.

Cutler, David M., Naomi E. Feldman, and Jill R. Horwitz. 2005. "U.S. Adoption of Computerized Physician Order Entry Systems." *Health Affairs*, vol. 24, no. 6 (November–December), pp. 1654–1663.

Department of Health and Human Services. 2008. *Budget in Brief: Fiscal Year 2009.* Available at www.hhs. gov/budget/09budget/2009BudgetInBrief.pdf.

Department of Veterans Affairs. 2008. *Medical Programs and Information Technology Programs: Congressional Submission, FY 2009,* vol. 2. Available at www.va.gov/budget/summary/2009/Volume_2-Medical_Programs_and information_Technology.pdf.

Eddy, David. 1990. "Practical Policies: Where Do They Come From?" *Journal of the American Medical Association,* vol. 263, no. 9 (March 2), pp. 1265–1275.

Evans, Dwight C., Paul W. Nichol, and Jonathan B. Perlin. 2006. "Effect of the Implementation of an Enterprise-Wide Electronic Health Record on Productivity in the Veterans Health Administration." *Health Economics, Policy, and Law*, vol. 1 (March 23), pp. 163–169.

Evans, R. Scott, and others. 1998. "A Computer-Assisted Management Program for Antibiotics and Other Antiinfective Agents." *New England Journal of Medicine*, vol. 338, no. 4 (January 22), pp. 232–238.

First Consulting Group. 2003. *Computerized Physician Order Entry: Costs, Benefits, and Challenges.* First Consulting Group. Available at www.fcg.com/research/ research-listing.aspx?rid=36&NoIntro=True.

Frisse, Mark E. 2006. "Comments on Return on Investment (ROI) as it Applies to Clinical Systems." *Journal of the American Medical Informatics Association*, vol. 13, no. 3 (May–June), pp. 365–367.

Gandhi, Tejal K., and others. 2005. "Outpatient Prescribing Errors and the Impact of Computerized Prescribing." *Journal of General Internal Medicine*, vol. 20, no. 9 (September), pp. 837–841.

Gans, David, and others. 2005. "Medical Groups' Adoption of Electronic Health Records and Information Systems." *Health Affairs*, vol. 24, no. 5 (September– October), pp. 1323–1333.

Garg, Amit X., and others. 2005. "Effects of Computerized Clinical Decision Support Systems on Practitioner Performance and Patient Outcomes: A Systematic Review." *Journal of the American Medical Association*, vol. 293, no. 10 (March 9), pp. 1223– 1238.

Garrido, Terhilda, and others. 2005. "Effect of Electronic Health Records in Ambulatory Care: Retrospective, Serial, Cross Sectional Study." *British Medical Journal*, vol. 330, no. 7491 (March 12), pp. 581–585.

Girosi, Federico, Robin Meili, and Richard Scoville. 2005. *Extrapolating Evidence of Health Information Technology Savings and Costs*. Santa Monica, Calif.: RAND Corporation.

George Washington University, Massachusetts General Hospital, and Robert Wood Johnson Foundation. 2006. *Health Information Technology in the United States: The Information Base for Progress*. Princeton, N.J.: Robert Wood Johnson Foundation. Available at www.rwjf.org/files/publications/ other/EHRReport 0609/pdf.

Grossman, Joy M., and Marie C. Reed. 2006. *Clinical Information Technology Gaps Persist Among Physicians*. Issue Brief No. 106. Washington, D.C.: Center for Studying Health System Change. November. Available at www.hschange.com/CONTENT/891/ 891.pdf.

Grossman, Joy M., and others. 2007. "Physicians' Experiences Using Commercial E-Prescribing Systems." *Health Affairs*, vol. 26, no. 3, Web Exclusive (April 23), pp. w393–404.

Han, Yong Y., and others. 2005. "Unexpected Increased Mortality After Implementation of a Commercially Sold Computerized Physician Order Entry System." *Pediatrics*, vol. 116, no. 6 (December), pp. 1506–15 12.

Harpole, Linda H., and others. 1997. "Automated Evidence-Based Critiquing of Orders for Abdominal Radiographs: Impact on Utilization and Appropriateness." *Journal of the American Medical Informatics Association*, vol. 4, no. 6 (November–December), pp. 511–521.

Harris, Lisa E., and others. 1998. "Effects of Multidisciplinary Case Management in Patients with Chronic Renal Insufficiency." *American Journal of Medicine*, vol. 105, no. 6 (December), pp. 464–471.

Hillestad, Richard, and others. 2005. "Can Electronic Medical Record Systems Transform Health Care? Potential Health Benefits, Savings, and Costs." *Health Affairs*, vol. 24, no. 5 (September–October), pp. 1103–1117.

Hing, Esther S., Catharine W. Burt, and David A. Wood- well. 2007. "Electronic Medical Record Use by Office- Based Physicians and Their Practices: United States, 2006." *Advance Data, National Center for Health Statistics*, no. 393 (October 26), pp. 1–7.

Honigman, Benjamin, and others. 2001. "Using Computerized Data to Identify Adverse Drug Events in Outpatients." *Journal of the American Medical Informatics Association*, vol. 8, no. 3 (May–June), pp. 254– 266.

Jha, Ashish K., and others. 2006. "How Common Are Electronic Health Records in the United States? A Summary of the Evidence." *Health Affairs*, vol. 25, no. 6, Web Exclusive (October 11), pp. w496–507.

Jha, Ashish K., and others. 2001. "Identifying Hospital Admissions Due to Adverse Drug Events Using a Computer-Based Monitor." *Pharmaco epidemiology and Drug Safety*, vol. 10, pp. 113–119.

Kaushal, Rainu, and others. 2006. "Return on Investment for a Computerized Physician Order Entry System." *Journal of the American Medical Informatics Association*, vol. 13, no. 3 (May–June), pp. 261–266.

Kibbe, David, and Steven Waldren. 2005. *Partners forPatients Electronic Health Record Market Survey*.

Leawood, Kan.: American Academy of Family Physicians and Center for Health Information Exchange. Available at www.centerforhit.org/PreBuilt/chit_2005p4pvendsurv.pdf.

Lindenauer, Peter K., and others. 2007. "Public Reporting and Pay for Performance in Hospital Quality Improvement." *New England Journal of Medicine,* vol. 356, no. 5 (February 1), pp. 486–496.

Linder, Jeffery A., and others. 2007. "Electronic Health Record Use and the Quality of Ambulatory Care in the United States." *Archives of Internal Medicine*, vol. 167, no. 13 (July 9), pp. 1400–1405.

McGlynn, Elizabeth, and others. 2003. "The Quality of Health Care Delivered to Adults in the United States." *New England Journal of Medicine*, vol. 348, no. 26 (June 26), pp. 2635–2645.

Mekhjian, Hagop S., and others. 2002. "Immediate Benefits Realized Following Implementation of Physician Order Entry at an Academic Medical Center." *Journal of the American Medical Informatics Association*, vol. 9, no. 5 (September–October), pp. 529–539.

Miller, Robert H., and Ida Sim. 2004. "Physicians' Use of Electronic Medical Records: Barriers and Solutions." *Health Affairs,* vol. 23, no. 2 (March–April), pp. 116– 126.

Miller, Robert H., and others. 2005. "The Value of Electronic Health Records in Solo or Small Group Practices." *Health Affairs*, vol. 24, no. 5 (September–October), pp. 1127–1 137.

Moshman Associates, Inc., and Booz Allen Hamilton. 2006. *Assessing the Economics of EMR Adoption and Successful Implementation in Physician Small Practice Settings.* Draft report prepared for the Office of the Assistant Secretary for Planning and Evaluation, Department of Health and Human Services.

Mullett, Charles J., and others. 2001. "Development and Impact of a Computerized Pediatric Antiinfective Decision Support Program." *Pediatrics,* vol. 108, no. 4 (October), pp. e75–e81.

Murray, Michael D., and others. 2004. "Failure of Computerized Treatment Suggestions to Improve Health Outcomes of Outpatients with Uncomplicated Hypertension: Results of a Randomized Controlled Trial." *Pharmacotherapy,* vol. 24, no. 3 (March), pp. 324–337.

National Center for Health Statistics, Centers for Disease Control and Prevention. 2007. *Health, United States, 2007,* Table 99.

Nebeker, Jonathan R., and others. 2005. "High Rates of Adverse Drug Events in a Highly Computerized Hospital." *Archives of Internal Medicine*, vol. 165, no. 10 (May 23), pp. 1111–1116.

Overhage, J. Marc, and others. 2001. "Controlled Trial of Direct Physician Order Entry: Effects on Physicians' Time Utilization in Ambulatory Primary Care Internal Medicine Practices." *Journal of the American Medical Informatics Association*, vol. 8, no. 4 (July–August), pp. 361–371.

Pan, Eric, and others. 2004. *The Value of Healthcare Information Exchange and Interoperability.* Wellesley, Mass.: Center for Information Technology Leadership.

Pizziferri, Lisa, and others. 2005. "Primary Care Physician Time Utilization Before and After Implementation of an Electronic Health Record: A Time–Motion Study." *Journal of Biomedical Informatics*, vol. 38, no. 3 (June), pp. 176–188.

Poissant, Lise, and others. 2005. "The Impact of Electronic Health Records on Time Efficiency of Physicians and Nurses: A Systematic Review." *Journal of the American Medical Informatics Association,* vol. 12, no. 5 (September–October), pp. 505–516.

Poon, Eric G., and others. 2004. "Overcoming Barriers to Adopting and Implementing Computerized Physician Order Entry Systems in U.S. Hospitals." *Health Affairs,* vol. 23, no. 4 (July–August), pp. 184–190.

Potts, Amy L., and others. 2004. "Computerized Physician Order Entry and Medication Errors in a Pediatric Critical Care Unit." *Pediatrics,* vol. 113, no. 1 (January), pp. 59–63.

Schoen, Cathy, and others. 2006. "On the Front Lines of Care: Primary Care Doctors' Office Systems, Experiences, and Views in Seven Countries." *Health Affairs*, vol. 25, no. 6, Web Exclusive (November 2), pp. w555–571.

Sequist, Thomas D., and others. 2005. "A Randomized Trial of Electronic Clinical Reminders to Improve Quality of Care for Diabetes and Coronary Artery Disease." *Journal of the American Medical Informatics Association*, vol. 12, no. 4 (July–August), pp. 431– 437.

Sittig, Dean F., and others. 2006. "Lessons from Unexpected Increased Mortality After Implementation of a Commercially Sold Computerized Physician Order Entry System." *Pediatrics*, vol. 118, no. 2 (August), pp. 797–801.

Subramanian, Usha, and others. 2004. "A Controlled Trial of Including Symptom Data in Computer-Based Care Suggestions for Managing Patients with Chronic Heart Failure." *American Journal of Medicine*, vol. 116, no. 6 (March 15), pp. 375–384.

SureScripts. 2007. *National Progress Report on E- Prescribing*. Alexandria, Va.: SureScripts. December.

Teich, Jonathan M., and others. 2000. "Effects of Computerized Physician Order Entry on Prescribing Practices." *Archives of Internal Medicine*, vol. 160, no. 18 (October 9), pp. 2741–2747.

Tierney, William M., and others. 2005. "Can Computer- Generated Evidence-Based Care Suggestions Enhance Evidence-Based Management of Asthma and Chronic Obstructive Pulmonary Disease? A Randomized, Controlled Trial." *Health Services* Research, vol. 40, no. 2 (April), pp. 477–497.

Tierney, William M., and others. 2003. "Effects of Computerized Guidelines for Managing Heart Disease in Primary Care: A Randomized, Controlled Trial." *Journal of General Internal Medicine*, vol. 18, no. 12 (December), pp. 967–976.

Tierney, William M., and others. 1988. "Computer Predictions of Abnormal Test Results: Effects on Outpatient Testing." *Journal of the American Medical Association,* vol. 259, no. 8 (February 26), pp. 1194–1198.

Tierney, William M., and others. 1987. "Computerized Display of Past Test Results: Effect on Outpatient Testing." *Annals of Internal Medicine*, vol. 107, no. 4 (October), pp. 569–574.

Upperman, Jeffrey S., and others. 2005. "The Introduction of Computerized Physician Order Entry and Change Management in a Tertiary Pediatric Hospital." *Pediatrics,* vol. 116, no. 5 (November), pp. e634–e642.

Walker, Jan, and others. 2005. "The Value of Health Care Information Exchange and Interoperability." *Health Affairs*, vol. 25, no. 6, Web Exclusive (January 19), pp. w5–10–18.

Wang, Samuel J., and others. 2003. "A Cost–Benefit Analysis of Electronic Medical Records in Primary Care." *American Journal of Medicine*, vol. 114, no. 5 (April 1), pp. 397–403.

In: Health Care Costs: Outlook and Options ISBN 978-1-60692-151-7
Editor: Raymond W. Inhurst, pp. 59-76

Chapter 2

THE LONG-TERM BUDGET OUTLOOK AND OPTIONS FOR SLOWING THE GROWTH OF HEALTH CARE COSTS*

Mr. Chairman, Senator Grassley, and Members of the Committee,

I appreciate the opportunity to appear before you to discuss the long-term fiscal outlook and approaches to addressing future budgetary imbalances.

Significant uncertainty surrounds long-term fiscal projections, but under any plausible scenario, the federal budget is on an unsustainable path—that is, federal debt will grow much faster than the economy over the long run. In the absence of significant changes in policy, rising costs for health care and the aging of the U.S. population will cause federal spending to grow rapidly. If federal revenues as a share of gross domestic product (GDP) remain at their current level, that rise in spending will eventually cause future budget deficits to become unsustainable. To prevent deficits from growing to levels that could impose substantial costs on the economy, revenues must rise as a share of GDP, or projected spending must fall—or some combination of the two outcomes must be achieved.

Future growth in spending per beneficiary for Medicare and Medicaid—the federal government's major health care programs—will be the most important determinant of long-term trends in federal spending. Changing those programs in ways that reduce the growth of costs—which will be difficult, in part because of the complexity of health policy choices—is ultimately the nation's central long-term challenge in setting federal fiscal policy. There may be ways, however, in which policymakers can reduce costs without harming the health of Medicare and

* Testimony. Statement of Peter R. Orszag Director, before the Committee on Finance United States Senate, dated June 17, 2008.

Medicaid beneficiaries. Our political system arguably is not particularly effective at addressing gradual long-term problems such as rising health care costs and aging. But the problems caused by rising health care costs are not just long-term ones. In fact, some of them are already having significant effects on various aspects of our society. Health care costs are already reducing workers' take-home pay to a degree that is both underappreciated and at least partially unnecessary, consuming roughly a quarter of the federal budget, and putting substantial pressure on state budgets (mostly through the Medicaid program), thereby constraining funding for other governmental priorities. Identifying and addressing inefficiencies in the nation's health care system can yield significant benefits, even in the short term, and focusing attention on those effects that are already occurring may be helpful in developing the consensus necessary to make the needed changes.

LONG-TERM PROJECTIONS OF SPENDING, REVENUES, AND DEBT

The Congressional Budget Office (CBO) projects that total federal Medicare and Medicaid outlays will rise from 4 percent of GDP in 2007 to 12 percent in 2050 and 19 percent in 2082—which, as a share of the economy, is roughly equivalent to the total amount that the federal government spends today. The bulk of that projected increase in health care spending reflects higher costs per beneficiary rather than an increase in the number of beneficiaries associated with an aging population. The aging of the population, though not the primary factor driving higher government spending in the future, will nonetheless exacerbate fiscal pressures. Future growth in spending on Social Security, for example, will largely reflect demographic changes; CBO projects that such spending will increase from about 4 percent of GDP today to 6 percent in 25 years and then will roughly stabilize at that rate thereafter. Under current policies, federal spending on programs other than Medicare, Medicaid, and Social Security—including national defense and a wide variety of domestic programs—is likely to contribute far less, if anything, to the upward trend in federal outlays as a share of GDP.

Long-term projections rely on numerous assumptions about economic and fiscal factors, and many different assumptions are possible. In The *Long-Term Budget Outlook* (December 2007), CBO presented two scenarios that are based on different assumptions about the federal budget over the next 75 years (see Table 1) [1]

Table 1. Assumptions About Spending and Revenue Sources Underlying CBO's Long-Term Budget Scenarios

	Extended-Baseline Scenario	Alternative Fiscal Scenario
	Assumptions About Spending	
Medicare	As scheduled under current law	Physician payment rates grow with the Medicare economic index (rather than using the lower growth rates scheduled under the sustainable growth rate mechanism)
Medicaid	As scheduled under current law	As scheduled under current law
Social Security	As scheduled under current law	As scheduled under current law
Other Spending Excluding Interesta	As projected in CBO's 10-year baseline through 2017, then remains at the projected 2017 level as a share of GDP	Remains at the 2007 share of GDP
	Assumptions About Revenue Sources	
Individual Income Taxes	As scheduled under current law inflation after 2007	2007 law with AMT parameters indexed for
Corporate Income Taxes	As scheduled under current law	As scheduled under current law
Payroll Taxes	As scheduled under current law	As scheduled under current law
Excise and Estate and Gift Taxes	As scheduled under current law	Constant as a share of GDP for the entire period
Other Revenues	As scheduled under current law through	As scheduled under current law through 2017;
	2017; constant as a share of GDP thereafter	constant as a share of GDP thereafter

Source: Congressional Budget Office.Notes: The extended-baseline scenario adheres closely to current law, following CBO's 10-year baseline budget projections from 2008 to 2017 and then extending the baseline concept in its projections for the rest of the years in the 75-year projection period, to 2082. The alternative fiscal scenario deviates from CBO's baseline projections even during the next 10 years, incorporating some changes in policy that are widely expected to occur and that policymakers have regularly made in the past. GDP = gross domestic product; AMT = alternative minimum tax.

[a]Federal spending on the refundable portions of the earned income tax credit and the child tax credit is not held constant as a percentage of GDP but is instead modeled with the revenue portion of the scenarios.

- The "extended-baseline scenario" adheres most closely to current law, following CBO's 10-year baseline for the first decade and then extending the baseline concept beyond that 10-year window [2]. The scenario's assumption of current law implies that many policy adjustments that lawmakers have routinely made in the past will not occur.
- The "alternative fiscal scenario" represents one interpretation of what it would mean to continue today's underlying fiscal policy. This scenario deviates from CBO's baseline even during the next 10 years because it incorporates some changes in policy that are widely expected to occur and that policymakers have regularly made in the past. Different analysts may perceive the underlying intention of current policy differently, however, and other interpretations are possible.

For decades, spending on Medicare and Medicaid has been growing faster than the economy, as has health care spending in the private sector. The rate at which health care costs grow relative to national income—rather than the aging of the population—will be the most important determinant of future federal spending. For its long-term projections, CBO assumed that even in the absence of changes in federal law, rates of spending growth in the Medicare and Medicaid programs would probably moderate to some degree [3]. As costs continue to rise, regulatory changes are likely at the federal level. At the state level, both legal and regulatory changes will probably occur; those changes would directly affect Medicaid, which is a joint federal–state program. And actions by employers, households, and insurance firms to slow the rate of health care cost growth in the private sector are likely to affect the public insurance programs to some extent. Nevertheless, spending for Medicare and Medicaid is likely to continue to grow faster than the economy over the long term.

Spending under the extended-baseline scenario would be somewhat lower than under the alternative fiscal scenario for two reasons. First, under the extended-baseline scenario's assumption that current law remains in place, the sustainable growth rate (SGR) mechanism for updating Medicare's payment rates for physicians would reduce those rates by about 4 percent or 5 percent annually for at least the next several years. However, since 2003, the Congress has acted to prevent such reductions. Therefore, for the alternative fiscal scenario, CBO assumed that those rates would grow with the Medicare economic index (which measures inflation in the inputs used for physicians' services). The difference in spending for Medicare under the two scenarios is less than 1 percent of GDP in all 75 years of the projection period.

A second and larger difference between the scenarios involves the assumption about other federal spending— that is, spending for programs other than Medicare, Medicaid, and Social Security but excluding interest on the public debt. Under the extended-baseline scenario, other federal spending in 2018 and later would equal about 7.7 percent of GDP, consistent with the projections for fiscal year 2017 in CBO's March 2007 baseline and projected levels of refundable tax credits. Under the alternative fiscal scenario, other spending during the projection period would remain about at its current level of 9.8 percent of GDP.

Spending for Medicaid and Social Security would be identical under both scenarios. In addition, both scenarios incorporate the assumption that the Medicare and Social Security programs will continue to pay benefits as currently scheduled, notwithstanding the projected insolvency of the programs' trust funds.

Despite those differences, under both scenarios total primary spending (all spending except interest payments on federal debt) would grow sharply in coming decades, CBO estimates, rising from its current level of 18 percent of GDP to more than 30 percent by 2082, the end of the 75-year period that CBO's long-term projections span (see Figure 1). If spending policy did not change and outlays did indeed grow to such levels relative to the economy, maintaining a sustainable budgetary path would require that federal taxation rise similarly. In the past half-century, total federal revenues have averaged 18 percent of GDP and peaked at nearly 21 percent, well below projected levels of future spending.

Ultimately, both scenarios involve an unsustainable fiscal path, but they differ significantly in their projections of revenues and in the extent and timing of substantial increases in federal debt:

- Under the extended-baseline scenario, revenues would reach substantially higher levels than have ever been recorded during the nation's history [4]. Under this scenario, the 2001 and 2003 legislation that lowered tax rates would expire as scheduled at the end of 2010, and the impact of the alternative minimum tax (AMT) would expand substantially over time (because its parameters, unlike most parts of the tax system, are not indexed to inflation) [5]. In addition, ongoing increases in real income (that is, income after an adjustment for inflation) would push taxpayers into higher income tax brackets. As a result, by 2082, federal revenues would reach 25 percent of GDP.

With the projected revenue increases and substantial reduction in other spending as a share of GDP embodied in this scenario, federal debt held by the public would fall relative to GDP until 2026.

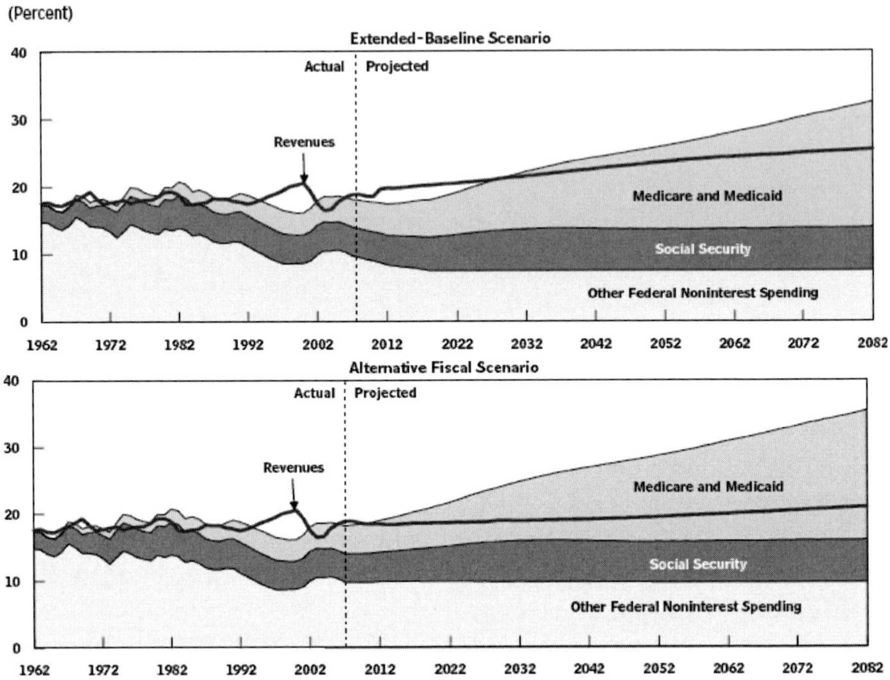

Source: Congressional Budget Office. *Note:* The extended-baseline scenario adheres closely to current law, following CBO's 10-year baseline budget projections from 2008 to 2017 and then extending the baseline concept in its projections for the rest of the years in the 75-year projection period, to 2082. The alternative fiscal scenario deviates from CBO's baseline projections even during the next 10 years, incorporating some changes in policy that are widely expected to occur and that policymakers have regularly made in the past.

Figure 1. Revenues and Spending Excluding Interest, by Category, as a Percentage of Gross Domestic Product Under CBO's Long-Term Budget Scenarios.

But after that, the combined effect of increased revenues and reduced spending for programs other than Medicare, Medicaid, and Social Security would be overwhelmed by growth in health care costs. Debt would start to climb, and if federal spending was allowed to grow as projected, policymakers would have to raise revenues further to keep the growth of debt from outpacing the growth of the economy (see Figure 2 and Table 2).

- Under the alternative fiscal scenario, by contrast, none of the changes to tax law scheduled after 2007 would take effect, and the AMT would be indexed to inflation. As a result, revenues would remain roughly constant as a share of GDP. The combination of roughly constant revenues and significantly rising expenditures would quickly create an unstable fiscal situation.

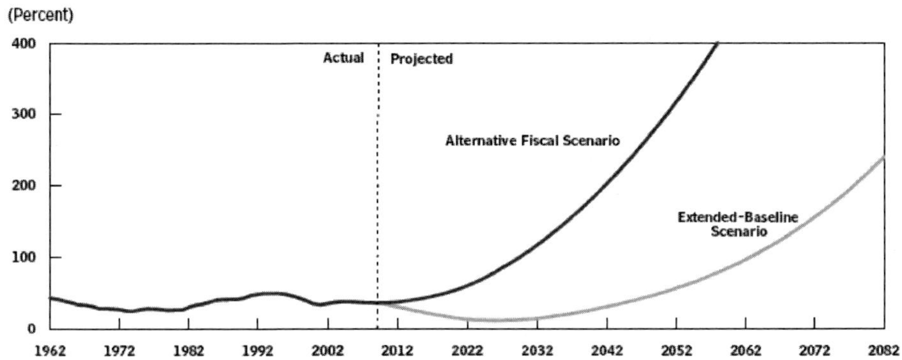

Source: Congressional Budget Office.

Note: The extended-baseline scenario adheres closely to current law, following CBO's 10-year baseline budget projections from 2008 to 2017 and then extending the baseline concept in its projections for the rest of the years in the 75-year projection period, to 2082. The alternative fiscal scenario deviates from CBO's baseline projections even during the next 10 years, incorporating some changes in policy that are widely expected to occur and that policymakers have regularly made in the past.

Figure 2. Federal Debt Held by the Public as a Percentage of Gross Domestic Product Under CBO's Long-Term Budget Scenarios.

A useful metric for the size of the adjustments in either spending or revenues required to avoid unsustainable increases in government debt is provided by the so-called fiscal gap. The gap measures the immediate change in spending or revenues necessary to generate a stable fiscal trajectory over a given period.

Under the extended-baseline scenario, the fiscal gap would amount to 0.6 percent of GDP through 2057 and 1.7 percent of GDP through 2082 (see Table 3). In other words, under that scenario, an immediate and permanent reduction in spending or an immediate and permanent increase in revenues of 1.7 percent of GDP—or an even.Under the alternative fiscal scenario, the fiscal gap would be much larger, amounting to 5.2 percent of GDP through 2057 and 6.9 percent through 2082.

Table 2. Spending and Revenues as a Percentage of Gross Domestic Product Under CBO's Long-Term Budget Scenarios

Percent	2007[a]	2030	2050	2082
	Extended-Baseline Scenario			
Primary Spending				
Social Security	4.3	6.1	6.1	6.4
Medicare[b]	2.7	5.6	8.9	14.8
Medicaid	1.4	2.5	3.1	3.8
Other noninterest	9.9	7.7	7.6	7.6
Subtotal, Primary Spending	18.2	21.8	25.7	32.5
Interest	1.7	0.6	2.3	11.0
Total Federal Spending	20.0	22.4	28.1	43.6
Revenues	18.8	21.4	23.5	25.5
Deficit (-) or Surplus				
Primary deficit (-) or surplus	0.5	-0.4	-2.3	-7.1
Total deficit	-1.2	-1.0	-4.6	-18.1
	Alternative Fiscal Scenario			
Primary Spending				
Social Security	4.3	6.1	6.1	6.4
Medicare[b]	2.7	5.9	9.4	15.6
Medicaid	1.4	2.5	3.1	3.7
Other noninterest	9.9	9.8	9.7	9.6
Subtotal, Primary Spending	18.2	24.2	28.3	35.3
Interest	1.7	4.8	13.6	40.1
Total Federal Spending	20.0	29.0	41.8	75.4
Revenues	18.8	18.9	19.4	20.9
Deficit (-) or Surplus				
Primary deficit (-) or surplus	0.5	-5.3	-8.9	-14.4
Total deficit	-1.2	-10.1	-22.5	-54.5

Source: Congressional Budget Office.

Note: The extended-baseline scenario adheres closely to current law, following CBO's 10-year baseline budget projections from 2008 to 2017 and then extending the baseline concept in its projections for the rest of the years in the 75-year projection period, to 2082. The alternative fiscal scenario deviates from CBO's baseline projections even during the next 10 years, incorporating some changes in policy that are widely expected to occur and that policymakers have regularly made in the past.

[a]. For 2007, numbers are actual and on a fiscal year basis.

[b].Spending for Medicare beneficiaries is net of premiums.

Table 3. The Federal Fiscal Imbalance Under CBO's Long-Term Budget Scenarios

Percentage of gross domestic product

Projection Period	Revenuess	Outlay	Fiscal Gap
	Extended-Baseline Scenario		
25 Years (2008-2032)	20.2	19.5	-0.7
50 Years (2008-2057)	21.3	21.9	0.6
75 Years (2008-2082)	22.1	23.8	1.7
	Alternative Fiscal Scenario		
25 Years (2008-2032)	18.6	21.4	2.8
50 Years (2008-2057)	18.8	24.1	5.2
75 Years (2008-2082)	19.2	26.1	6.9

Source: Congressional Budget Office.

Note: The extended-baseline scenario adheres closely to current law, following CBO's 10-year baseline budget projections from 2008 to 2017 and then extending the baseline concept in its projections for the rest of the years in the 75-year projection period, to 2082. The alternative fiscal scenario deviates from CBO's baseline projections even during the next 10 years, incorporating some changes in policy that are widely expected to occur and that policymakers have regularly made in the past.

THE EFFECTS OF RISING FEDERAL DEBT ON THE ECONOMY

Growth in debt is not necessarily a problem. As long as the economy is also expanding just as fast and interest rates are stable, the ratio of debt to GDP and the share of GDP that must be devoted to paying interest on the debt will remain stable. Under CBO's long-term projections, deficits of about 1.4 percent of GDP would result in a stable ratio. Moreover, even if debt grows faster than GDP for a limited time, difficulties do not always arise.

But sustained and rising budget deficits would absorb funds from the nation's pool of savings and reduce investment in the domestic capital stock and in foreign assets. As capital investment dwindled, the growth of workers' productivity and of real wages would gradually slow and begin to stagnate. As capital became scarce relative to labor, real interest rates would rise. In the near term, foreign investors would probably increase their financing of investment in the United States, which would help soften the impact of rising deficits on productivity in the United States. However, borrowing from abroad would not be without its costs.

Over time, foreign investors would claim larger and larger shares of the nation's output, and fewer resources would be available for domestic consumption.

Under both the extended-baseline and alternative fiscal scenarios, growing budget deficits and the resulting increases in federal debt could lead to slower economic growth. The effects would be most striking under the alternative fiscal scenario: Debt would begin to climb rapidly and would reach roughly 300 percent of GDP by 2050. In CBO's estimation, that rising federal debt would reduce the capital stock—compared with what it would be if deficits were held to their share of the economy in 2007—by 40 percent in 2050 and would lower real gross national product by 25 percent [6]. Although the outlook for the economy under the extended-baseline scenario would be more auspicious in the near term, over the long run, rising deficits would also lead to significant economic harm.

Differences between the economic costs of one policy for achieving long-term fiscal sustainability and those of another are generally modest in comparison with the costs of allowing deficits to grow to unsustainable levels. In particular, the difference in economic costs between acting to address projected deficits (by either reducing spending or raising revenues) and failing to do so is generally much larger than the cost implications of pursuing one approach to deficit reduction rather than another. Nonetheless, a policy of reducing the growth of spending would in general impose smaller macroeconomic costs than one of increasing tax rates, although the economic effects would depend in part on the specific measures that were adopted.

Policy Options to Constrain Future Spending on Health Care

The most significant cause of future long-term spending growth—health care costs—is also particularly complicated to address. Policymakers face both challenges and opportunities in trying to reduce those costs. Over long periods, cost growth per beneficiary in the Medicare and Medicaid programs has tended to track cost trends in private-sector markets for health care. Many analysts therefore believe that significantly constraining the growth of costs for Medicare and Medicaid is possible only in conjunction with slowing the growth of costs in the health sector as a whole.

A variety of evidence suggests that opportunities exist to constrain costs without adversely affecting health outcomes—and even perhaps to simultaneously reduce cost growth and improve health. So a central challenge will be to restrain the growth of costs without harming the incentives to provide appropriate care and develop valuable new treatments. Moving the nation toward that possibility—which will inevitably be an iterative process in which policy steps are tried, evaluated, and perhaps reconsidered—is essential to moving the country toward a sounder long-term fiscal footing.

Increasing the Salience of Costs and Improving Efficiency

One factor perpetuating inefficiencies in health care is a lack of clarity regarding the cost of health insurance and who bears that cost, especially employment-based health insurance. Employers' payments for employment-based health insurance and nearly all payments by employees for that insurance are excluded from individual income and payroll taxes. Although both theory and evidence suggest that workers ultimately finance their employment-based insurance through lower take-home pay, the cost is not evident to many workers.

Workers may demand less efficiency from the health system than they would if they knew the full cost that they pay via forgone wages for coverage or if they knew the actual cost of the services being provided. Making the underlying costs associated with employment-based insurance more transparent might prove to be quite important in containing health care costs. For workers and dependents with employment-based insurance, deductibles and copayments account for only about a fifth of their health care spending. The remainder comes from insurance premiums, only a quarter of which is paid directly by workers. If transparency increases and workers see how much their income is being reduced for employers' contributions and what those contributions are paying for, there might be a broader change in cost-consciousness that shifts demand.

Generating More Information About

Effectiveness and Changing Incentives. Straightforward changes to the Medicare and Medicaid programs—such as more stringent eligibility criteria, greater cost sharing, or changes in payments to providers—could reduce federal spending in part by shifting costs from the federal government to households or other sectors. Efforts to control federal spending alone would have some effect but would be most sustainable to the extent that they succeeded in constraining cost growth in the rest of the health care system.

The general consensus among health economists is that the large increase in health care spending over the past several decades was principally the result of the emergence of new medical technologies and services and their adoption and widespread diffusion by the U.S. health care system (see Table 4) [7]. Advances in medical science have made available to patients and physicians a wealth of new medical therapies, many unheard of in even the relatively recent past. Some of the advances permit the treatment of previously untreatable conditions, introducing new categories of spending. Others, relative to older modes of treatment, improve medical outcomes at added cost, expanding existing spending.

Table 4. Estimated Contributions of Selected Factors to Growth in Real Health Care Spending per Capita, 1940 to 1990

(Percent)	Smith, Heffler, and Freeland (2000)	Cutler (1995)	Newhouse (1992)
Aging of the Population	2	2	2a
Changes in Third-Party Payment	10	13	10b
Personal Income Growth	11–18	5	<23
Prices in the Health Care Sector	11–22	19	*
Administrative Costs	3–10	13	*
Defensive Medicine and Supplier-Induced Demand	0	*	0
Technology-Related Changes in Medical Practice	38–62	49	>65

Source: Congressional Budget Office based on Sheila D. Smith, Stephen K. Heffler, and Mark S. Freeland, "The Impact of Technological Change on Health Care Cost Increases: An Evaluation of the Literature" (working paper, 2000); David M. Cutler, "Technology, Health Costs, and the NIH" (paper prepared for the National Institutes of Health Economics Roundtable on Biomedical Research, September 1995); and Joseph P. Newhouse, "Medical Care Costs: How Much Welfare Loss?" Journal of Economic Perspectives, vol. 6, no. 3 (Summer 1992), pp. 3–22.

Notes: Amounts in the table represent the estimated percentage share of long-term growth that each factor accounts for.

< = less than; > = greater than; * = not estimated.

[a.] Represents data for 1950 to 1987.

[b]. Represents data for 1950 to 1980

Future increases in spending could be moderated if costly new medical services were adopted more selectively in the future than they have been in the past and if the diffusion of existing costly services was slowed. Although that approach would mean fewer medical services, evidence suggests that savings are possible without a substantial loss of clinical value. Currently, the added clinical benefits of new medical services are not always weighed against added costs before those services enter common clinical practice. And newer, more expensive services are sometimes used in cases in which older, cheaper alternatives could offer comparable outcomes for patients.

Two potentially complementary approaches to reducing total spending on health care—rather than simply reallocating spending among different sectors of the economy—involve generating more information about the relative effectiveness of medical treatments and changing the incentives for providers and consumers of health care. In addition to those changes, a variety of approaches to changing health-related behavior could improve health outcomes at a given level of costs.

The current financial incentives for both providers and patients tend to encourage or at least facilitate the adoption of expensive treatments and procedures, even if evidence about their effectiveness relative to existing therapies is limited. Costly services that are known to be highly effective for some types of patients are sometimes provided to others for whom clinical benefits have not been rigorously demonstrated. More information on the "comparative effectiveness" of alternative medical treatments could offer a basis for ensuring that future technologies and existing costly services are used only in cases in which they confer clinical benefits that are superior to those of other, cheaper services [8].

To affect medical treatment and reduce health care spending, the results of comparative effectiveness analyses would ultimately have to change the behavior of doctors and patients—that is, to get them to use fewer services or less intensive and less expensive services than are currently projected. Bringing about those changes would probably require action by public and private insurers to incorporate the results into their coverage and payment policies in order to affect the incentives for doctors and patients.

The Medicare program has not taken costs into account in determining what services are covered and has made only limited use of data on comparative effectiveness in its payment policies; but if statutory changes permitted it, Medicare could use information about comparative effectiveness to promote higher-value care. For example, Medicare could tie its payments to providers to the cost of the most effective or most efficient treatment. If that payment was less than the cost of providing a more expensive service, then doctors and hospitals would probably elect not to provide it—so the change in Medicare's payment policy would have the same practical effect as a coverage decision. Alternatively, enrollees could be required to pay for the additional costs of less effective procedures (although the impact on incentives for patients and their use of care would depend on whether and to what extent they had supplemental insurance coverage that paid some or all of Medicare's cost-sharing requirements).

Even in the absence of more information about comparative effectiveness, changes in incentives could help control health care costs, but such measures would be more likely to maximize the health gains obtained for a given level of spending if they were combined with improved information. On the provider side, greater bundling of payments to cover all of the services associated with a treatment, disease, or patient could reduce or eliminate incentives to provide additional services that might be of low value. Such approaches, however, might raise concerns about the financial risk that providers faced and about their incentives to provide too little care. On the consumer side, a landmark health insurance experiment by RAND showed that higher cost sharing reduces spending—particularly when compared with a plan offering free care—with few or no adverse effects on health [9]. However, compared with more typical health insurance plans (which do not offer free care), high-deductible designs have more modest effects on health care spending; such approaches also raise concerns about the financial burden on people with significant health problems (again reflecting trade-offs between providing insurance protection and maintaining incentives to control costs) [10].

Adopting Measures to Promote Healthier Living

Finally, the ultimate objective of any health care system is to promote health, whether by treating diseases that arise or by preventing them from occurring in the first place. Despite the cost of the nation's health care system, many concerns exist about the degree to which it is attaining that objective. Indeed, concerns about rising health care costs might not be so prominent if more evidence showed that those expenditures were yielding commensurate gains in health. In part, those shortcomings in the system's performance relate to the concerns noted above about whether patients are receiving the most effective or most cost-effective treatments—reflecting a lack of information, among other factors. Concerns also exist, though, about steps that are not being taken today to prevent the onset of disease, even when clear evidence is available about their benefits. Proposals that encourage more prevention and healthy living can help promote better health outcomes, although their net effects on federal and total health care spending are uncertain. Moreover, bringing about substantial changes in behavior could require actions outside the formal health care sector, and even then might be very difficult to achieve.

Nonetheless, policy changes could encompass preventive measures and efforts to encourage healthier lifestyles. Broadly speaking, three basic policy approaches could be adopted. First, more information about the consequences of unhealthy behavior or the factors contributing to it could be made available, in forms that could affect individual behavior or even social norms. (Nutritional information, for example, is readily available for packaged foods but more difficult to come by for other sources, such as restaurant meals). Second, financial incentives could be modified to encourage healthier living and to discourage unhealthy activities.

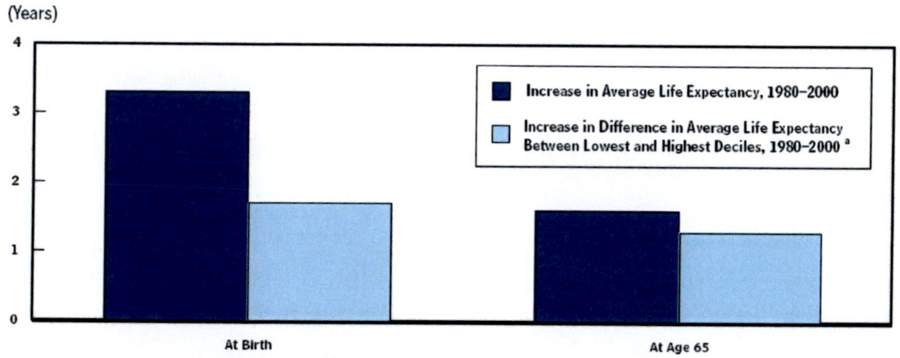

Source: Congressional Budget Office using data from Gopal K. Singh and Mohammad Siahpush, "Widening Socioeconomic Inequalities in U.S. Life Expectancy, 1980–2000," International Journal of Epidemiology, vol. 35, no. 4 (2006), pp. 969–979; and National Center for Health Statistics, Health, United States, 2007 (Hyattsville, Md., 2007), Table 27.

[a] Socioeconomic groups are defined using county-level indicators of education, occupation, unemployment, wealth, income, and housing conditions.

Figure 3. Increase in Life Expectancy, and Increase in Difference in Life Expectancy by Economic Status.

For example, cigarette taxes could be increased, which would discourage smoking, especially among teenagers. While those two types of measures are necessary and valuable, recent evidence suggests that a third approach could prove to be the most important channel for affecting health behavior: Default options in various realms could be established, and other steps could be taken to encourage healthy behavior and discourage poor health habits [11].

In terms of their health, less educated and poorer groups exhibit worse behaviors and have worse outcomes than do more educated and richer groups. For example, less advantaged groups smoke more and have higher rates of obesity. That observation raises the issue of whether well- designed defaults could help to narrow the differences in health behaviors. If so, defaults may also help to reduce the growing gap in life expectancy by education and income (see Figure 3) [12]

What sorts of defaults may matter? As just one example, a growing body of research demonstrates that eating habits are strongly affected by the environment and presentation [13]. About 20 percent of Americans participate in federal nutrition programs, so restructuring those programs could have a considerable effect [14]. The school lunch program, in which governments can determine the food served to children, may be most amenable to presentational changes. But related strategies could be adopted for other federal nutrition programs, such as the Women, Infants, and Children program and the Supplemental Nutrition Assistance Program, formerly called the Food Stamp program.

CBO's Activities

Because future health care spending is the single most important factor determining the nation's long-term fiscal condition, CBO is devoting increasing resources to assessing options for reducing such spending in the future. The agency has expanded the number of fulltime-equivalent staff analyzing health care issues from 30 at roughly this time last year to 44 now, with 6 more coming on board within the next four months. Last year, CBO established a panel of health advisers (experts from academia, industry, and independent research organizations), which meets periodically to examine frontier research in health policy and to advise the agency on its analyses of health care issues. As part of its work generally, CBO continually reviews research conducted both in and outside of government. Late this year, the agency plans to release two reports on health policy: One will present budget estimates for numerous specific policy options, and the other will address critical topics related to proposals to make major changes in the health care system. We hope these efforts will be of significant value to the Congress and to this Committee in assessing ways to address these critical policy issues.

REFERENCES

[1] The projections in this testimony are taken from that report and do not reflect subsequent changes in law or in CBO's 10-year baseline.

[2] CBO's baseline is a benchmark for measuring the budgetary effects of proposed changes in federal spending or revenues. The projections of budget authority, outlays, revenues, and the deficit or surplus that it comprises are calculated according to rules set forth in the Balanced Budget and Emergency Deficit Control Act of 1985.

[3] See Congressional Budget Office, *The Long-Term Outlook for Health Care Spending* (November 2007).

[4] The projections that make up CBO's baseline are not intended to be predictions of future budgetary outcomes; rather, they represent CBO's best judgment of how economic and other factors would affect federal spending and revenues if current laws and policies remained in place.

[5] The AMT is a parallel income tax system with fewer exemptions, deductions, and rates than the regular income tax. Households must calculate their tax liability (the amount they owe) under both the AMT and the regular income tax and pay the larger of the two amounts.

[6] The capital stock consists of businesses' equipment and structures as well as housing. Gross national product (GNP) measures the income of residents in the United States after deducting net payments to foreigners. Gross domestic product, by contrast, measures the income that is generated by the production on U.S. soil, including the production that is financed by foreign investors. Because rising deficits can increase borrowing from foreigners, GNP is a better measure of the economic effects of deficits than is GDP.

[7] Congressional Budget Office, *Technological Change and the Growth of Health Care Spending* (January 2008).

[8] For a discussion of comparative effectiveness, see Congressional Budget Office, *Research on the Comparative Effectiveness of Medical Treatments: Issues and Options for an Expanded Federal Role* (December 2007).

[9] See Willard G. Manning and others, "Health Insurance and the Demand for Medical Care: Evidence from a Randomized Experiment," *American Economic Review*, vol. 77, no. 3 (June 1987), pp. 25 1–277.

[10] See Congressional Budget Office, *Consumer-Directed Health Plans: Potential Effects on Health Care Spending and Outcomes* (December 2006).

[11] See Peter R. Orszag, Director, Congressional Budget Office, "Health Care and Behavioral Economics: A Presentation to the National Academy of Social Insurance" (Washington, D.C.: May 29, 2008).

[12] Congressional Budget Office, *Growing Disparities in Life Expectancy* (April 17, 2008).

[13] See Brian Wansink, *Mindless Eating: Why We Eat More Than We Think* (New York: Bantam Dell, 2006).

[14] David R. Just, Lisa Mancino, and Brian Wansink, "Could Behavioral Economics Help Improve Diet Quality for Nutrition Assistance Program Participants?" (U.S. Department of Agriculture, Economic Research Service, Economic Research Report No. 43, June 2007).

In: Health Care Costs: Outlook and Options
Editor: Raymond W. Inhurst, pp. 77-84
ISBN 978-1-60692-151-7

Chapter 3

HEALTH COSTS AND HEALTH INFORMATION TECHNOLOGY*

Congressional Budget Office

HEALTH INFORMATION TECHNOLOGY (HEALTH IT)

Applications of health IT can enable providers to deliver better-quality health care more efficiently by:

- Eliminating medical transcription and physical management of files
- Prompting prescription of generic rather than brand-name drugs
- Reducing duplication of diagnostic tests
- Reminding physicians of appropriate preventative care
- Identifying drug interactions and allergies

But the cost implications of health IT depend on context:

- Health IT is "necessary but not sufficient" to generate savings

- Financial incentives
- Use of information
- Toaster analogy

---

* Congressional Budget Office, Presentation to the Alliance for Health Reform, Peter Orszag, Director, June 20, 2008.

Federal Spending under CBO's Alternative Fiscal Scenario

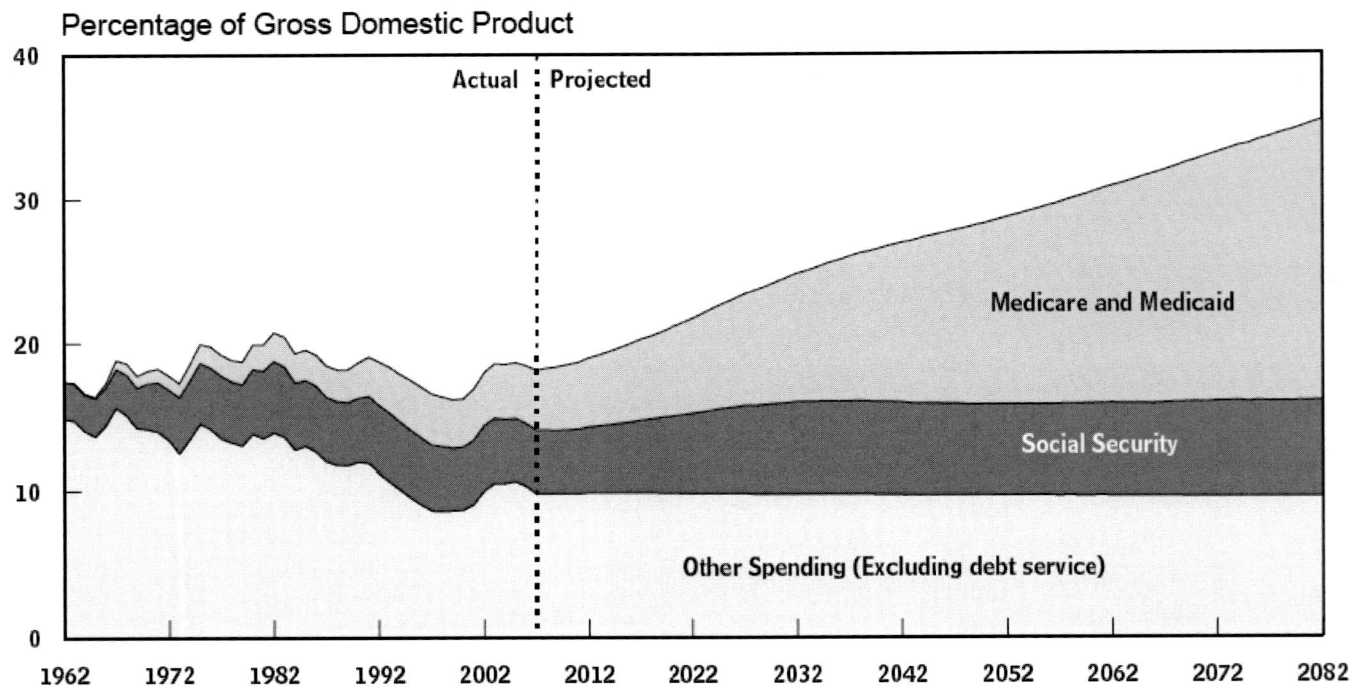

Estimated Contributions of Selected Factors to Long-Term Growth in Real Health Care Spending per capita, 1940 to 1990

	Smith, Heffler, and Freeland (2000)	Cutler (1995)	Newhouse (1992)
Aging of the Population	2	2	2
Changes in Third-Party Payment	10	13	10
Personal Income Growth	11-18	5	<23
Prices in the Health Care Sector	11-22	19	Not Estimated
Administrative Costs	3-10	13	Not Estimated
Defensive Medicine and Supplier-Induced Demand	0	Not Estimated	0
Technology-Related Changes in Medical Practice	38-62	49	>65

Sources of Growth in Projected Federal Spending on Medicare and Medicaid

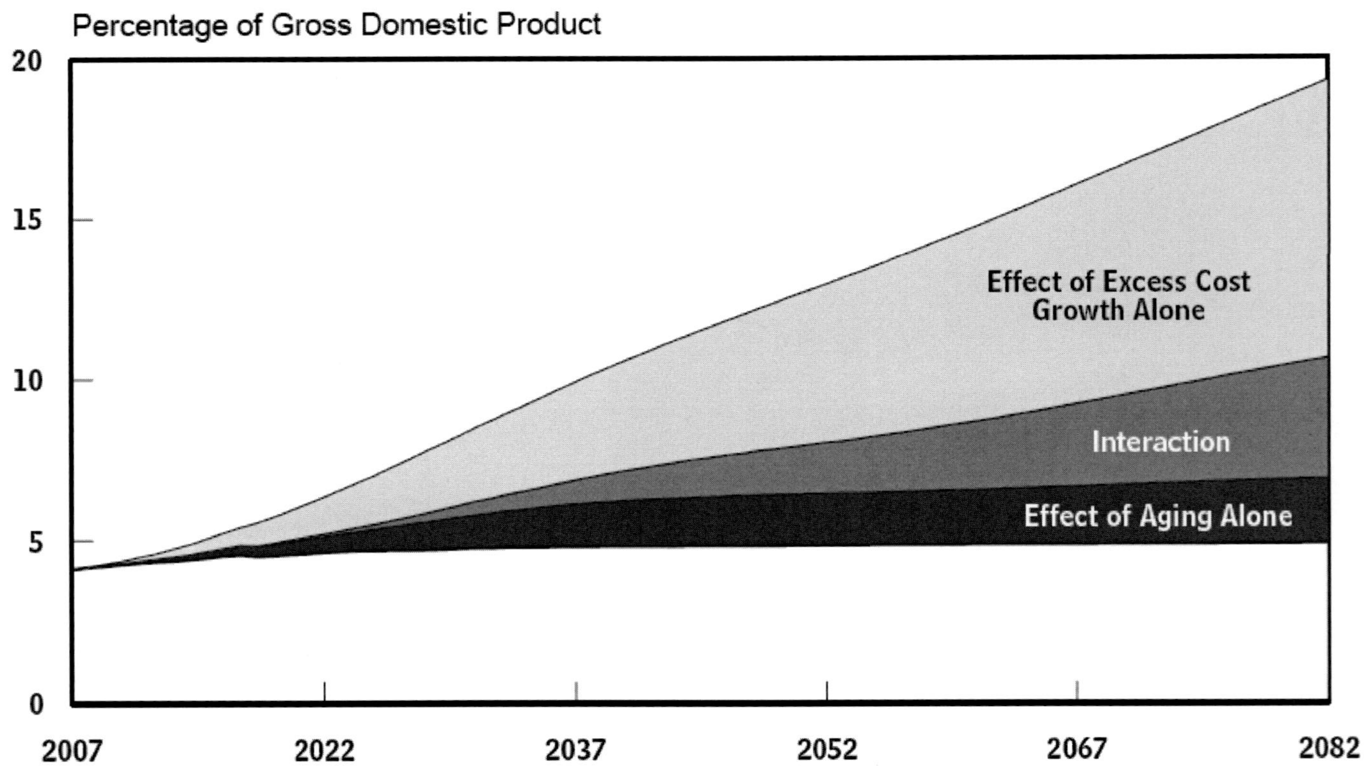

Medicare Spending per Beneficiary in the United States, by Hospital Referral Region, 2005

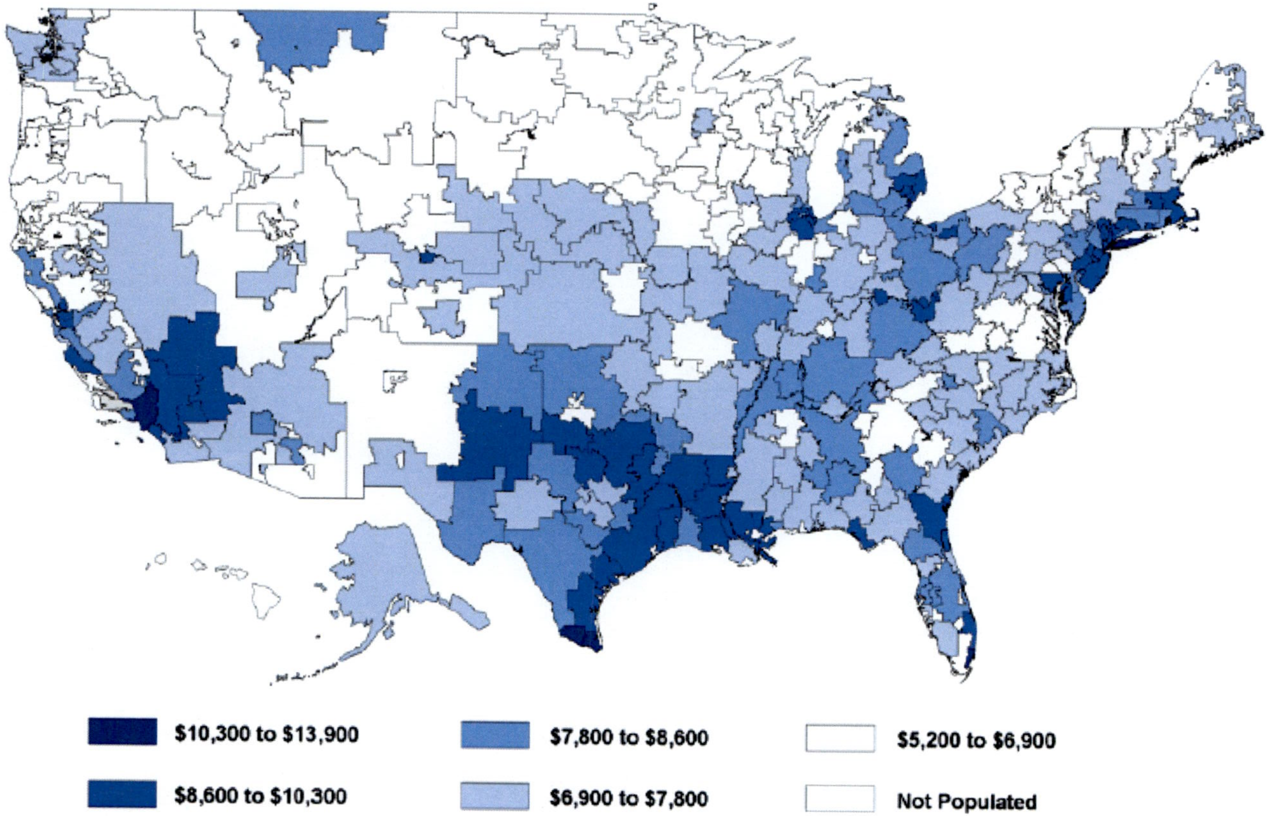

Variations among Academic Medical Centers

Use of Biologically Targeted Interventions and Care-Delivery Methods Among Three of U.S. News and World Report's "Honor Roll" AMCs

	UCLA Medical Center	Massachusetts General Hospital	Mayo Clinic (St. Mary's Hospital)
Biologically Targeted Interventions: Acute Inpatient Care			
CMS composite quality score	81.5	85.9	90.4
Care Delivery—and Spending—Among Medicare Patients in Last Six Months of Life			
Total Medicare spending	50,522	40,181	26,330
Hospital days	19.2	17.7	12.9
Physician visits	52.1	42.2	23.9
Ratio, medical specialist / primary care	2.9	1.0	1.1

Source: Elliot Fisher, Dartmouth Medical School.

– Health IT applications are most promising in integrated health systems

Untapped Resource: Health IT Could Have Critical Role in Comparative Effectiveness Research

- Widespread use of health IT applications could make large sets of data on care and outcomes available for comparative effectiveness research
- Health IT systems could aid in implementing and tracking changes in care based on research findings

The RAND Corporation Study

- RAND estimated $80 billion in net annual savings potentially attributable to Health IT adoption
- Examined potential rather than likely impact
- Considered only studies demonstrating positive effects from implementation of Health IT systems
- Did not consider growth in adoption under current law when calculating savings

Policies to Promote Health IT Systems

Mechanisms to promote the use of health IT

- Subsidies for adopting new technologies
    - Induces those who are "close" to adopting
- Penalties for failing to use health IT system
- Requirement to use health IT

INDEX

A

B

C

D

E

I

J

L

M

N

O

U

V

W

Y